CAN WE STILL CALL HER WILD?

The question, conservation never dared to ask.

CAN WE STILL CALL HER WILD?

The question, conservation never dared to ask.

MONISH KUMAR KUPENDRA

Clever Fox® PUBLISHING
Chennai • Bangalore

CLEVER FOX PUBLISHING
Chennai, India

Published by CLEVER FOX PUBLISHING 2025

ISBN: 978-93-6707-931-7

CONTENTS

FOREWORD

I have known Monish for over six years as a friend, field companion, and someone whose conservation journey I've closely witnessed. From volunteering in animal rescues to participating in rigorous wildlife expeditions, his path into ecology wasn't planned, but felt driven by curiosity, care, and a deep connection to conservation.

Can We Still Call Her Wild? is his first book, written not as a professional author, but as someone compelled to tell a story that matters. In over four months, Monish has crafted a fictional narrative that brings together the life of a female Asian elephant and the experiences of five zoology students in the field. The elephant calf, born free and later orphaned, finds herself relocated to a semi-captive elephant camp. Her gradual shift to life in human-managed conditions raises unsettling but important questions about captivity, care, and the idea of "wildness".

Alongside her story, the journey of the students sheds light on the raw realities of field research, its challenges, ethical dilemmas, and transformative power. Their experiences mirror the transition many young conservationists go through, from romantic notions of wildlife to a more grounded, complex understanding shaped by direct engagement.

This book stands out for its honesty. It doesn't preach; it invites. It's for anyone who wants to think more deeply about conservation and the role we play in it. I believe it will resonate with students, researchers and curious readers alike.

Kishore Raj D *(MSc)*
Ashoka Trust for Research in Ecology and the Environment
Bengaluru
July 2025

THE MATING AND THE MIRACLE

The Chikkagundi Elephant Camp in Karnataka was no stranger to stories of the wild. Nestled on the threshold of rolling grasslands and damp deciduous forests, it was a sanctuary of half-freedom, a twilight space where elephants like Veera lived between two worlds: the wild and the watched.

Semi-captive elephants such as Veera are typically released into the forest at night to allow natural foraging and interaction before being brought back to camp each morning.

Veera was 34 years old in the July of 2000, a majestic tusker with streaked temples, weather-worn tusks, and an air of silent authority. That July, something changed.

The 12th of the month dawned warm and golden. The monsoon had washed the land clean weeks earlier, leaving behind a flush of fresh grass and a thousand scents floating on the wind. That evening, as twilight crept over the treetops, Veera wandered deeper than usual. It was then that one of the trackers, who would later recall the moment vividly, saw him approach a herd of wild elephants grazing quietly near the forest edge.

Veera moved cautiously but with intent. The first female he encountered, an older cow, showed no interest. Veera extended his trunk, drawing scent from her hindquarters and vaginal opening, and performed what researchers call the "urine test", curling the tip of his trunk into his mouth to analyze hormone levels. She was not in estrus. He moved on.

A few meters ahead stood another female, younger perhaps 22 to 26 years old. She paused as Veera approached. He repeated the urine test and this time, her scent revealed what he was looking for, she was in estrus.

The reproductive cycle of an elephant consists of two main stages: the follicular phase and the luteal phase. The follicular phase typically spans 4 to 6 weeks and concludes with estrus, a brief period lasting 4 to 6 days during which the female is fertile and receptive to mating. Ovulation occurs within this estrus window, making it the only time when mating can lead to conception. Following estrus, the cycle enters the luteal phase, which lasts between 6 and 12 weeks. During this phase, the female is not fertile and will not engage in mating. If conception does not occur, the cycle restarts with a new follicular phase.

Veera's behavior shifted immediately. He raised his head and gently reached his trunk over her shoulder, then along her flank, inhaling deeply. He followed her closely, walking in synchrony for hundreds of meters, occasionally releasing low-frequency rumbles which are inaudible to the human ear but felt in the ground. These infrasonic calls are part of elephant courtship and communication, often traveling kilometers through the earth.

He was not aggressive. His movements were calm and observant. When the female paused near a muddy wallow, Veera circled to her rear, then gently rested his chin across her rump, for which she did not resist. Instead, she stood firm which is a clear signal of receptiveness. With care, he mounted her. The act was short, lasting less than a minute, but it was deliberate, acknowledged by both.

Interestingly, the other females in her herd did not interfere. They stood at a respectful distance, observing without hostility. Elephants, especially females within a matriarchal group, are selective and protective, but in this case, they seemed to accept Veera's approach. It may have been his calm demeanor, his lack of aggression, or simply the unspoken knowledge shared among elephants that this union was part of something greater, an instinctive rhythm older than memory.

The trackers, curious and quietly awed, named her Sumangali, "the auspicious one." They kept an eye on her, noting the days she grazed near the camp, the slow change in her body, the way her gait shifted as weeks melted into months. *For 22 months the longest known gestation of any land mammal*, Sumangali carried the promise of that July inside her.

The early rains came in the spring of 2002. On a heavy, cloud-draped evening, with lightning hissing at the far edges of the sky, the herd gathered on the open grassland not far from camp. There was only one tree in that wide field, an old teak that had stood sentinel for decades. Beneath it, Sumangali began to sway.

The signs were unmistakable to her sisters. Her breathing changed, her tail lifted, and she began to vocalize a deep, rolling rumble that carried a note of effort and vulnerability. The herd encircled her instinctively. Six elephants, her kin, her protectors formed a living wall around her, their trunks resting gently against her flanks.

Then came the drama of birth.

Elephants rarely give birth under the open sky unless they trust the space and the company. As the first tremors of labor began, the clouds broke open above, drenching the earth in a heavy, silver rain. Thunder rolled across the grasslands. Yet in that moment, the forest held its breath.

A chorus of chirps and guttural bellows rose from the herd, short, high-pitched squeals of excitement, infrasonic rumbles of reassurance, trumpets of alertness. These were not just noises, but they were communications layered with meaning. *Elephants produce a wide range of vocal sounds, from deep infrasonic rumbles to sharp, high-pitched trumpets, which are capable of traveling several kilometers.* During birth, their calls became a symphony of solidarity.

Sumangali bent her knees and let her massive body lower to the muddy grass. With a final bellow, the calf emerged wet, motionless, enshrouded in the thick, white veil of placenta. For one breathless moment, there was only silence. Then, a tiny trunk tore through the membrane.

The calf gasped its first breath as thunder cracked overhead.

Sumangali turned, trembling with exhaustion, and wrapped her trunk around her daughter. The herd moved in, trunks reaching, touching and blessing. One cow began to nudge the calf gently to stand. Another scooped mud over the afterbirth, masking the scent from predators which is an observed behavior among mammals to protect the newborn.

The calf's legs wobbled beneath her, yet she rose dripping, blinking and alive.

From the trees beyond the field, unseen by the elephants, a forest tracker watched with a heart too full for words. He scribbled one note in his book, "*Born in rain. Like a blessing.*"

And so, in 2002, under the storm-heavy sky and the trembling teak tree, a new life entered the world. The daughter of Sumangali and Veera. The one whose story was only just beginning.

BETWEEN GIANTS AND GATEWAYS

A month had passed since the herd moved deeper into the forest. The calf, still new to the world, had already learned to walk in the shadows of giants. Her tiny frame followed her mother's every step, guided by touch, scent, and sound and guarded by the silent gaze of the Matriarch.

Far from where the herd wandered, in the dusty corridors of Aranya Bhavana in Mysuru, another story began to take shape.

Five MSc Zoology students namely Rishi, Sukhanya, Ananth, Nethra, and Surya from a university in Mysuru, stood anxiously at the office of the Deputy Conservator of Forests (DCF), Mysuru Wildlife Division, clutching a printed proposal. Their research project aimed to study the protective behavior of an elephant mother and calf, comparing patterns between forest interiors and fringing zones. It was a unique idea, born of curiosity and deep respect. But the DCF, having seen too many well-meaning yet inexperienced researchers drift into danger, declined their request. Without formal wildlife fieldwork or credentials, the answer was a firm no.

Disheartened but not defeated, the group regrouped that evening in the university library. Among them, Rishi, a quiet, observant, and deeply driven team member, remembered an old friend named Ibrahim. A city-bred classmate, pampered from childhood, who had never set foot in a forest but whose uncle served as an Assistant Conservator of Forests in Mysuru.

Rishi hesitated. He knew Ibrahim's softness, his obsession with clean sheets and city lights. But desperation builds unlikely bridges. He made the call.

To Rishi's surprise, Ibrahim was intrigued, not for the science, but for the prospect of "roaming with elephants." Still, he agreed to speak with his uncle.

A week passed with anxious waiting. Then, news arrived. Ibrahim returned with a spark in his voice saying that his uncle was willing to meet the team and possibly refer them to the DCF. He believed the project might even benefit the department.

But there was a catch.

"If you get permission," Ibrahim grinned, "I come with you to see the forests and elephants."

Rishi's inner voice sighed. "*You won't last a night in the wild, brother*". But he nodded. Ibrahim was their only bridge for now.

Eight days later, a call came from Ibrahim. "Tomorrow, 2 PM. Meet at the ACF's office. He's heading to the field to meet the DCF in order to inspect elephant-proof trenches. You'll have to tag along and talk there."

Sleep evaded all five that night. Excitement buzzed louder than forest cicadas. By 2 PM the next afternoon, dressed in simple field gear, the team gathered outside the ACF's office. After brief introductions, they climbed into the forest jeep. As the city slipped away, the ACF explained the day's schedule that a field inspection at a sensitive boundary zone is happening, joined by other officers and a wildlife scientist.

The jeep rumbled along a rugged track, jostling its passengers over humps and hollows. The canopy grew thicker, the air cooler and the landscape showcased its guars and sambar deer here and there. The Chikkagundi range was alive, wild and quiet.

The site was tense. A notorious elephant had been breaching the trench line to raid nearby farmlands, prompting this visit. The DCF was already on-site, deep in discussion.

But fate had its own script.

As the students stepped out of the jeep, their eyes widened. The scientist beside the DCF was none other than the guest lecturer who had once visited their college for a session on elephant conservation that only a few students had dared to engage in. He recognized them immediately. Smiling, he turned to the DCF and whispered something.

The DCF, now connecting the dots, the same students whose proposal he had rejected, now backed by both an ACF and a recognized academic, paused and listened.

Suddenly, all focus on the trench shifted toward the students.

The ACF briefly outlined their project and its potential value for long-term monitoring. Meanwhile, the scientist and students walked a short distance along the trench's edge, where they explained the plan in detail, documenting a mother-calf pair over three years, observing maternal protection behavior as the calf grew.

When they rejoined the group, the DCF asked, "How long will this project run?"

"Three years," Rishi replied. "Until the calf becomes a juvenile."

"And how do you define that transition?" the DCF tested.

Without hesitation, Sukhanya responded. "When the calf's height crosses the belly line of the mother, it's considered a juvenile and that's when the suckling becomes difficult at that stage."

The scientist smiled remembering that exact point had come from his guest lecture.

The DCF gave a slow nod. "Meet me at my office next Friday. By then, I'll have contacted the ranges to check if any recent calf births have been recorded. If a suitable site is identified, you'll get your approval."

That week, Aranya Bhavan came alive with communication. Range Forest Officers from across the division called in, reporting herds, calves, and behavioral observations. Among them, Rajappa, the RFO of Chikkagundi, stood out. His call confirmed something special. A known semi-captive tusker, Veera, had mated with a wild female, recently seen with a newborn calf. Trackers had confirmed sightings during patrol.

When Friday arrived, the team waited nervously in the office. As the DCF was in a meeting about trench reinforcements, they were called in after 30 minutes.

He handed them a hand written list of ranges with potential study sites.

They didn't hesitate. "Chikkagundi," said Nethra, eyes lighting up. "That's the one."

"It's a rare case," Surya added. "A semi-captive mating with a wild female. It's a bridge between two different management systems. It could add value to our study."

The DCF raised an eyebrow. "You want Chikkagundi?"

"Yes, sir. It offers deeper insight."

Without a word, he turned to his assistant. "Prepare the permission letter. Inform all Chikkagundi staff that this team has my full backing but on one condition, quarterly progress reports, and a direct six-monthly review, either here or at the site. Also," he added firmly, "no field movement alone. A tracker and driver must accompany the team at all times" and accommodation and food at the Chikkagundi elephant camp itself."

A formal email followed shortly after, marked to the entire team, ibrahim's uncle, and the scientist.

With that, the field study was no longer just a dream.

The team immediately contacted their two sponsors who were Mr. Vinay, a dedicated wildlife photographer and Mrs. Susan, a city rescuer from Bengaluru. Both passionate conservationists who had agreed to support the project.

They now had the place, the people, and the permission.

The forest had opened its gates.

But just as the wheels began to turn, a new challenge quietly emerged...

BENGALURU, BISIBELEBATH AND THE BIG REVEAL.

With the time passing by, the team had just one major task left, which was gathering the essential camping gear. Mr. Vinay, their sponsor, had recommended a small shop in Shivajinagara, Bengaluru. It was an old haunt of his, and he had assured them that the shopkeeper would take care of everything and that he would settle the payment later.

So, one misty morning, they boarded a bus from Mysuru to Bengaluru. The journey was not long but jerky, punctuated by laughter and speculation about the days ahead. After getting down at the Satellite Bus Stand, they caught a city bus to Majestic, then another to Shivajinagara.

A few hundred meters of walking later, they stood in front of a curious old store. The windows were fogged with time, and the signboard creaked with each gust of wind. Piles of dusty gear leaned against old wooden racks. It was everything a city shop shouldn't be, but exactly what they needed.

Sukhanya wrinkled her nose and questioned herself "*Was it really necessary to come all the way from Mysuru for this?*"

But she quickly reminded herself that it was sponsored.

As her expression betrayed her thoughts, the old shopkeeper, a wiry man in his 70s with eyes sharper than a field knife, gave a knowing smile. "Don't judge the shop, miss," he said. "Just tell me what you need. I'll give you the best gear."

That single line changed the air in the room.

With hopeful glances exchanged, the team began reading out their list. But the shopkeeper raised a hand and growled, "One person speaks. Rest keep quiet."

Startled, they all turned to Rishi, who took charge.

"Five pairs of gum boots, raincoats, field bags, and wide-brimmed hats," he said calmly.

The shopkeeper nodded and asked for their shoe sizes. One by one, they replied. Within five minutes, he had laid out every item they'd asked for which were clean, sturdy, and brand new, despite being wrapped in dust-covered packaging. Sukhanya's eyes widened in disbelief.

"All this… 670 rupees," the old man said, brushing his palms together.

Rishi mentioned Mr. Vinay, and the man smiled. "Yes, he already informed me. Take them. And walk carefully to the bus stand as this area isn't as friendly as it looks."

Following his warning, they had Ananth carry the sack of gear on his shoulder while the rest surrounded him like a security detail. They made it to the bus stand without incident and caught a direct bus to Majestic, then back to Satellite, and finally returned to Mysuru.

It was a long journey which was nearly 5 hours round-trip. But as they stepped off the final bus, a new problem awaited.

They all headed to Ananth's house, which was closest to the bus stop. His mother greeted them with a warm smile, until her eyes fell on the dusty sack.

"What is this?" she asked, puzzled.

The other four turned toward Ananth.

He hadn't told his parents.

With a sheepish smile, Ananth finally blurted out, "Amma... we're going to the forest. It's for our project... we'll have to stay there for some time... maybe near elephants."

"No!" came her immediate response. "No jungle! No elephants! Are you mad?"

A deep silence settled over the living room.

Before anyone could speak, Ananth's father stepped out. "What's all this noise?"

Ananth's mother responded before anyone else could. "Your son is going into the jungle behind elephants with his friends!"

Even his father frowned. "You've lost your mind."

Rishi stepped forward gently. "Uncle, we've received formal permission from the DCF. Even a scientist is involved. This isn't a casual trip, it's official."

Those two words, the DCF and the scientist worked like magic. Ananth's father blinked, looked at the sack, and slowly nodded. "If it's officially approved, then... fine."

The room relaxed. The team turned to Ananth, exhaling in relief.

"Why didn't you tell them earlier?" Nethra asked, exasperated.

Ananth shrugged. "They wouldn't have agreed. I thought... I'll tell them once everything's ready."

With a half-smile and a lot of nervous energy, his mother sighed, "Will you all have breakfast before leaving at least?"

"Of course!" said Ananth.

She served them steaming plates of BisiBeleBath with crispy Kara Boondi on the side which is one of Karnataka's proudest comfort meals. As they ate, the team laughed, chattered, and finally felt like a real unit.

After breakfast, they left the sack at Ananth's house and headed to a nearby coin-operated phone booth to call Mr. Vinay. He'd already heard from the shopkeeper and wished them luck, telling them to call if they needed anything else.

From there, it was straight to the university library. They created planning sheets, sketched out two data collection tables with neat black lines and red-ink headings. Roles were assigned, observation formats were finalized and excitement was finally overtaking the chaos.

The next day, they returned to the DCF's office, eager to report their readiness. The assistant recognized them and waved them into the cabin.

The DCF looked up with a smile. "All set to enter the forest?"

"Yes sir. Thank you, sir!" all five responded in unison.

The officer appointed to monitor their project entered the room. After a brief discussion, the DCF informed them they could head to Chikkagundi Camp the following Monday, as there was some work going on in the range that week.

They agreed to report at the range office by 11 a.m., and the DCF nodded. Instructions were passed to the assistant and the officer to prepare accommodations and local staff coordination.

Then came a surprising gesture, the DCF insisted on taking a group photo with them. As they posed, he tried handing over ₹50 each, saying, "For good luck. Buy yourselves something usefull."

They refused at first. Then, hesitantly, accepted with smiles.

As they left the office, Nethra whispered to the rest, "*Why is the DCF doing all this? We were the ones who asked him… not the other way around". Then the whole team raised their shoulders as a gesture of not knowing about it started walking together.*

Back at the library, they found Ibrahim wandering near the entrance, pestering the librarian. The moment he saw Rishi, he broke into a wide grin and hugged him.

"When are we leaving?" he asked.

Rishi sat him down. "Ibrahim, the forest isn't a picnic spot. It's monsoon and it'll rain day and night. You can't expect hotels or clean restrooms."

"But then," Ibrahim asked, confused, "how will you all manage in that?"

Rishi gave a tired smile. "Because we're not there for comfort. We're there to learn."

Ibrahim lowered his voice. "I could've just asked my uncle to take me… but that's not what I want. I want to understand forests, elephants and I want to be with you all."

His honesty softened Rishi.

"Okay," he said finally. "Tell your uncle. If he agrees, maybe we can bring you in on the second or third day, once we settle in."

The others nodded.

With only four days left before departure, the team dispersed, each with responsibilities, lists, excitement, and a little fear. The real journey hadn't even begun, and already the forest was testing them in small ways.

The gear was ready. The minds were set. And somewhere deep in Chikkagundi, Sumangali and the herd wandered, unaware that five determined students were coming their way, not to chase them, but to understand their world.

DUNG AND DESTINATION

The much-awaited Monday finally arrived. At the break of dawn, with a drizzle lacing the Mysuru skies, the team gathered at Ananth's house, just as planned the night before. His mother, half-concerned and half-proud, served them a steaming, heavy breakfast, akki rotti, coconut chutney, and piping-hot filter coffee. She fussed over their packed bags and reminded them for the fifth time to wear the raincoats, not to wander without the staff and call home whenever they found a coin booth.

"Stay together," said Ananth's father, handing him a folded ₹50 note with quiet seriousness.

With hearts pounding and gear in hand, the five of them boarded the Mysuru–Chikkagundi bus, squeezing into the back row with their dusty sack full of equipment and thick field notebooks wrapped in plastic covers. Conversation was a mix of excitement and nerves.

At exactly 10:50 AM, they got off at the Chikkagundi bus stop. The smell of wet mud and burning firewood from a roadside tea shop lingered in the air. Across the road stood a worn-out forest department jeep.

Out stepped a lean man, khaki shirt slightly faded but perfectly pressed. His face was lined, sharp, and alert.

"I'm Rajappa, the Range Forest Officer," he said, extending a firm hand.

The team introduced themselves with wide smiles and respectful nods.

“You want to have some tea?” he offered, gesturing toward the shop.

“We’re good, sir. We had a heavy breakfast,” Ananth replied.

“Alright, let’s move then,” Rajappa said, motioning them toward the jeep.

As they clambered in, the driver, a cheerful man in his early twenties, turned around and offered his hand with a wide grin. “Shiva,” he said, “your driver for today.”

The jeep rattled to life, coughing slightly as it rolled forward. The road was uneven and damp from recent rains. Within five minutes, they reached the Range Forest Office, a low-slung structure nestled beneath tall teak trees.

“Why are we stopping here, sir? Why not go straight to the campsite?” Nethra asked, genuinely curious.

Rajappa glanced back. “The tracker who’s been monitoring the herd is waiting here. You’ll need him with you from now on.”

Stepping out of the jeep, they noticed a man waiting on the veranda, about 50 years old, with a thick, proud mustache, wearing a slightly oversized camouflage uniform and carrying a double barrel gun and a weathered notebook.

Rajappa introduced him, “This is Gangayya. He’ll be your tracker until the project ends. Knows the forest better than anyone.”

Gangayya gave them a sharp salute and a small smile. “I’ll walk with you till you walk out.”

He seemed serious, seasoned and yet genuinely excited about their presence.

Nearby stood a second jeep, dirt-streaked and ready for rough roads.

Rishi looked around. "Where's the driver, sir?"

Gangayya smirked. "Gone to smoke his beedi. Should be here soon."

Just then, a slightly disheveled man emerged from behind a nearby wall, brushing ash off his hands. His face carried the look of someone caught mid-break.

"Baala, sir. Sorry I'm late," he said quickly, lighting breath heavy with leftover beedi smoke.

He shook everyone's hands casually and added, "Don't worry sir, I've driven elephants and many officers through this forest. You're safe."

With introductions complete, the expedition finally came together, one jeep, a trusted tracker, one rugged driver, and five eager students and plenty of motivation and dedication.

They loaded their gear and waved goodbye to Shiva and the staff at the office.

Now, the forest awaited.

The road soon narrowed into a slushy track, weaving deeper into the dense Chikkagundi forest. To reach their camp, they had to cross two separate forest sections, thick with bamboo, lantana, and the scent of last night's rain.

In the back of the jeep, Nethra and Surya were slowly slipping into naps, rocked by the jeep's rhythmic bumps, while the others remained wide-eyed, craning their necks to catch any movement in the undergrowth.

Suddenly, Gangayya's hand shot up.

"Stop, stop, stop!" he said urgently.

Baala hit the brakes.

Everyone froze, darting their eyes between the trees.

"What happened?" whispered Sukhanya.

"Dung," Gangayya said, pointing ahead.

A few meters ahead, on the muddy trail, was a fresh pile of elephant dung.

"Want to check it, sir?" Gangayya asked Rishi with a small grin.

"Yes! Let's go," said Rishi, the rest of the team instantly alert.

They remembered the lecture clearly, the one where their visiting scientist taught them how elephant digestion could be studied through dung analysis. It wasn't just waste but it was data.

Asian elephants (Elephas maximus) exhibit relatively low digestive efficiency, typically assimilating only 20–45% of the fibrous plant material they ingest. This limitation arises from their classification as non-ruminant hindgut fermenters, wherein microbial fermentation of cellulose occurs primarily in the caecum and large intestine rather than in a foregut chamber, as seen in ruminants. Consequently, a substantial proportion of lignocellulosic material remains undigested and is expelled in the feces, resulting in dung that is visibly rich in coarse plant fibers.

Before moving closer, Gangayya warned, "Check your surroundings. If the dung is fresh, they might still be nearby."

Scanning the trees and bamboo clumps, they slowly stepped toward the pile. The air smelled sweet and earthy, and a crow cawed distantly.

Picking up a fallen stick, Rishi gently cracked open one of the dung boluses.

"It's warm," whispered Surya.

Baala, leaning out from the jeep, murmured, "Very fresh."

Gangayya crouched and examined the contents.

"Ragi fibres," said Gangayya, pointing at the long strands.

Baala nodded. "Yes. This elephant might have raided a ragi field."

Excited, the team scribbled notes, labeled the sample, and asked Gangayya to record the GPS coordinates, which he did on his handheld unit.

This was their first real field data. Their first smell of the wild beyond stories and lectures.

With spirits high, they climbed back into the jeep.

"Still excited?" Baala chuckled.

"Now more than ever," said Surya.

The road ahead grew rougher and 20 more minutes of bumps, mud, and stunning silence, interrupted only by birdcalls and the occasional rustle of leaves.

Finally, they reached a clearing tucked inside the forest, surrounded by towering trees and thick undergrowth. A few small structures, one cement, some tin-roofed, and one thatched hut, made up the Chikkagundi elephant camp.

Smoke from a firewood stove curled into the sky. A mahout in a lungi walked past carrying a football sized Ragi ball, nodding at the new arrivals.

Children peeked from behind one of the huts, giggling and whispering.

"Where do we stay, sir?" asked Nethra.

Baala pointed to a stone building with two rooms. "That's yours. No fan, one solar lantern and clean mattresses."

Perfect.

They dropped their bags, quickly freshened up, and hurried back toward Gangayya, who stood near the jeep checking his notebook.

Without missing a beat, Rishi asked the one question burning in all their minds.

"Sir… can we see Veera?"

Gangayya's lips curled into a half-smile.

"Veera and his mahout have gone into the forest to collect fresh branches for the night," he said, wiping a speck of mud from his boot with a stick.

"Why not just let him graze inside?" Surya asked curiously.

Gangayya looked up with a knowing expression. "He's in musth right now. We don't let him roam at night during this time as its too risky. It'll take at least a couple of weeks before he settles."

That word *musth*, rang a bell. All of them had read about it, studied it, but hearing it here, in the field, gave it weight.

Musth is a periodic, hormonally-driven condition characterized by significant behavioral and physiological changes in adult males, typically commencing between 15 to 20 years of age. The condition is marked by elevated androgen concentrations, particularly testosterone, resulting in heightened aggression, increased sexual activity, temporal gland hypertrophy with viscous secretion, and continuous urine dribbling. Musth episodes can persist for several weeks to months and are generally observed on an annual basis, although variation exists based on individual health, age, and social hierarchy. From a reproductive perspective, musth confers a selective advantage, as females in estrus preferentially mate with males in this state, likely due to the association with higher fitness and dominance. The behavioral manifestations during musth, including reduced affiliative interactions and increased agonistic encounters, have critical implications for both in situ and ex situ elephant management.

"But don't worry," Gangayya added, softening his voice. "They'll be back soon. The mahout never strays far from the camp when Veera's in this state."

He looked at their muddy feet, rain-flecked shirts, and tired yet excited eyes and asked "Why don't you all go freshen up?" he offered. "We'll have some jaggery tea ready by the time you're done. Strong, forest tea. You'll need it."

The team nodded, still absorbing the weight of what they'd just learned. They turned toward their quarters, walking with a little more reverence for the forest and for Veera, the unseen giant who was already shaping their story without even being present.

The scent of boiling tea leaves soon drifted through the camp, mingling with the smell of damp earth.

And deep in the forest, somewhere among the trees and shadows, Veera stood tall, tugging fresh branches with his powerful trunk, unaware that five eager minds had arrived to his camp.

FIRST FOOTPRINTS

The quarters smelled of wood polish and earth, and the faint echo of cicadas buzzed in the background. As the team settled down inside, metal trays clanged in the kitchen down the hallway. A few minutes earlier, they'd walked into the camp still carrying dust from the road. But now, freshened up and finally seated with hot glasses of tea, the moment felt surreal.

Each of them wrapped their fingers around the glass tumbler, taking in the scent, tea leaves, jaggery, hints of tulsi, and something indefinably local. The first sip made all five pause.

Surya's eyes widened. That was no ordinary tea.

They looked at each other, astonished and amused. It was as though the forest itself had brewed it.

"We have to ask for the recipe," Surya added, "and give it to our parents. I'll tell mine to make this every morning, half asleep or not."

"It's sorted," Nethra grinned, leaning back. "This is going to be our staple. We're here for what, six months? A year? Its more than two years."

They laughed, the kind of laughter that rises out of tired joy and shared novelty. The forest air drifted in through the window, soft and damp, and it all suddenly felt real. They were here, not in a classroom or lab, but in the living, breathing jungle, on the edge of the unknown.

After their tea and light-hearted banter, the team walked out in search of Gangayya. They found him near the equipment shed, talking to another forest worker.

"Sir," Nethra asked, "can you give us a short tour of the camp, please?"

Gangayya smiled, and nodded. "Surely, *magale*," he said kindly. "That means daughter in Kannada."

The camp was modest with sturdy structures made from local timber and corrugated roofs. The smell of neem, smoke, and elephant dung lingered in the air. Gangayya began walking them around, pointing out each structure: the elephant kitchen, the supply hut and the staff quarters. First, he introduced the camp elephants, most of them born and raised in the camp where each had its own story. A younger elephant named Nandi swung her trunk playfully at a crow. An older female, Mothi, stood silently under a mango tree, her eyes half-closed in the midday heat.

"They are like family," Gangayya said. "Some of them know this camp better than we do."

Then, they came to a more somber sight, a large kraal built from thick eucalyptus trunks, each as wide as a man's chest. Inside stood a powerful tusker, pacing slowly. His eyes were dark and restless. One of his ears had a small tear, possibly from an old fight. His skin bore fresh wounds telling history of his recent capture.

"That elephant was caught near Bandipura," Gangayya said. "He kept breaking fences. Went too far with the raids. They had to bring him here."

The team fell silent. A mahout was offering a tight knot of hay through the gaps, and another man stood beside him with a long stick, its end wrapped in sponge. He dipped it into a bottle and gently dabbed the elephant's side.

Sukhanya stepped a little closer. "What are they doing, sir?"

"Applying medicine, during capture, there are often injuries. And the hay, it calms him. Makes him feel he's not alone." Gangayya replied.

The elephant's trunk curled and uncurled, occasionally brushing the kraal wall.

"Can we talk to the mahouts?" Surya asked.

Gangayya considered their expressions, they were curious but cautious, their faces a mix of awe and hesitation. "Later," he said gently. "Once you're more used to being here. Let them finish their work. The elephant needs calm right now."

They nodded. They had seen elephants before, in festivals. But here, it was different. Here, they were wild hearts in wooden cages.

Gangayya led them away, along a trail towards a nearby water body. "Come, I'll show you where the elephants bathe."

The trail curved through sal and jamun trees, with lantana choking the undergrowth. The air was alive with cicadas, and a langur's sharp bark echoed somewhere above. As they approached the bathing area which was a large, natural pond ringed by muddy banks.

Nethra stopped mid-step. "Do you hear that?"

Everyone froze. On the opposite side of the water, thick lantana bushes rustled, not like wind, but like something moving deliberately. The kind of movement that carried weight.

They watched in silence. From within the green chaos, the tip of an elephant's trunk poked out, snaking through the air.

A heartbeat later, his head emerged.

"A wild tusker," Rishi whispered, but before anyone could respond, Surya shouted, "A wild tusker! Gangayya, over here!"

The massive figure pushed through the lantana, revealing tusks, ears, and a load of cut tree branches cradled between his trunk and tusks.

"That's Veera," Gangayya said, now running towards them. "He's back."

"Where's his mahout?" Sukhanya asked, scanning the bushes.

"Walking beside him, probably. This thick lantana hides everything," Gangayya said.

Sure enough, a moment later, a man in a dusty shirt appeared beside Veera and began climbing onto his back as the tusker stepped into the pond.

Veera moved slowly, with practiced ease, his legs half-submerged in the water. He seemed unbothered by the group watching him from the bank.

Within two minutes, Veera crossed the pond. The team instinctively stepped back, giving him room. He stepped onto dry land, gently placed the branches down, and his mahout dismounted.

A kavadi came forward, carrying thick iron chains. With practiced speed, he wrapped Veera's front legs. The elephant stood still with calm.

"He's in musth," Gangayya explained. "Even though he's calm, we can't take risks. So we chain him like the others. It's for safety."

The mahout walked toward the group and greeted them with folded hands. "Namaskara, madam," he said, looking at Sukhanya.

"This is Zubair," Gangayya said. "He's Veera's mahout."

Zubair nodded. "Veera was a crop raider near H.D. Kote. We captured him during his twenties. He took time… but now, he listens."

"Even during musth?" Rishi asked.

Zubair smiled. "Yes. He has a calm mind."

Their curiosity naturally shifted.

"What about the herd?" asked Nethra. "The one we're supposed to study?"

Gangayya's tone changed. "They've been moving. We've named the mother elephant as Sumangali. It's been a week since we last saw her."

"Will we get to see them?"

"Of course," Gangayya nodded. "We'll leave early. I'll cook rice and sambar, pack it for lunch. The forest is dense. You'll need energy."

"Are you ready with your gear?" he asked.

The team exchanged excited nods. "Yes, sir!"

As the camp was surrounded with dense canopy, mosquitoes had begun their relentless humming . Veera stood still, swaying gently, trunk lifting now and then, as if trying to remember the scent of the new arrivals.

"He's sniffing us," Rishi whispered.

Sukhanya stepped closer, her eyes on Veera. "I want to touch his trunk someday."

"You will," said Gangayya. "But slowly. Let him learn your smell first."

The day's weight was beginning to settle in their bones. Gangayya told them to rest as tomorrow would be long. The team headed back to their quarters discussing about the wild herd.

Inside, they washed their feet, pulled out notebooks, and sat cross-legged again.

"I can't believe we saw Veera," Nethra said.

"He's huge," Surya added. "And calm. That mahout has a bond with him."

Sukhanya was quiet, then spoke softly. "I was scared. But I wanted to stay there and understand him."

"We're here mainly for the wild ones," Rishi reminded them. "Veera's part of this place now, but out there, a calf is learning to walk. That's who we're here for."

Silence fell for a while, broken only by the occasional buzz of a mosquito or the distant rumble of Veera shifting his weight in the distance.

It was their first full day in the jungle.

But only the first footprints had been made.

THE FIRST DAY

The sun had not yet risen when the call of a distant peacock pierced the still air. It was their first real morning in the forest, and the silence of dawn hung thick over Chikkagundi. Inside the forest quarters, the students were already stirring. Anantha, half-awake, was fumbling for his field boots while Surya stood outside brushing his teeth, staring into the golden-blue horizon. The cool air carried the earthy scent of damp mud and leaf litter, a fragrance so raw and grounding that it felt a world apart from the Mysuru mornings they were used to.

By 7:30 a.m., the five students were assembled quietly at the entrance of the range quarters. Each wore light camouflage or khaki-colored clothing, hats pulled snug, and field boots firmly laced. Around their shoulders hung notebooks, GPS units, and one old camera slung in rugged cases. Rishi adjusted his strap and looked around, the forest was beginning to glow under the touch of soft sunlight, the shadows still long and the breeze still gentle.

Gangayya arrived shortly after, holding a folded map and a long wooden stick, its edges worn smooth from years of guiding, tapping, and pointing through the undergrowth.

"Today, we'll walk," he said in a tone both commanding and calm. "There's an old dry water body not far from here. Good spot. They come there early sometimes."

Soon after their breakfast, baala drove them to the edge of the trail in the jeep. As the group got down and gathered their gear,

Gangayya walked over to him and gave instructions, “Pick us up at 4 PM,” he said, “near the coconut grove.”

Baala nodded, revved the engine, and drove off slowly, leaving behind a light cloud of dust and the fading rumble of the jeep as it disappeared around a bend in the forest.

With that, their walk began.

The forest was slowly waking up, stirred by streaks of sunlight filtering through towering Arjuna and Shorea trees. The canopy danced gently in the early breeze, and the light played across the forest floor in golden patches. Twigs crackled underfoot and the air carried the faint scent of decaying wood and fresh grass. Every now and then, Gangayya would stop, crouch, and run his fingers along the ground, tracing broken twigs, flattened grass, or bark peeled from a tree trunk, reading the silent signs of life that most eyes would have missed. The students followed closely, careful with each step, their senses sharpening with every moment as their boots met the leaf-littered floor.

“See this?” Gangayya said, pointing at a pile of fresh dung, still moist, with fibrous green strands curled on top. “This is less than twelve hours old. A small herd passed by sometime late last night.”

Nethra immediately scribbled in her field journal, while Sukhanya bent down to examine a large circular footprint nearby. The edges were rounded, and faint toenail impressions could still be seen in the soft mud.

“That’s a front leg,” she whispered, recalling the diagrams and sketches from their guest lecture.

They continued along a narrow trail that hugged the contours of a small forest stream. Bird calls rang out above and around them, gossiping jungle babblers flitting from branch to branch, and the sudden wingbeat of a grey hornbill cutting across the canopy in a blur. No one spoke. There was no need to. The forest filled the space between them with its sounds, the soft rustle of wind, the lazy flicker of a leaf, and the rhythmic crunch of boots pressing into the dry earth.

About an hour into their walk, Gangayya slowed down, raising his hand subtly. Up ahead lay a wide, hollow depression. It was an old water body, now long dry. The basin stretched out like a shallow crater, bare and cracked, with thick lantana bushes crowding the far end and coarse grasses scattered along the rim. The students stayed on the elevated boundary, a natural ledge about ten feet above the basin floor.

Just as they were about to step forward, Surya whispered, "There."

Four elephants stood at the far end of the basin, three full-grown females and a juvenile male, his tiny tusks poking out from either side of his trunk like small white crescents. All four were alert with their ears spread wide, trunks raised slightly in mid-air, their posture stiff and upright, as if sensing something invisible yet familiar.

Netra scanned carefully. Her gaze lingered, searching for distinct marks or shapes. Then she whispered, "Not Sumangali's herd. No calf."

The group crouched quietly behind a thicket of thorny bushes along the rim. The elephants below weren't feeding, but they were standing in a semi-circle, protective and focused, the juvenile nestled in the middle while their tails flicked back and forth with agitation.

And then, beyond them, from inside the lantana thicket, something moved.

Quick, low and blood-stained.

Three rusty-colored dholes, wild dogs of the forests in India, emerged, tugging violently at the hind leg of a spotted deer carcass. The flesh was torn, ribs exposed, blood darkening the already dry mud beneath. One of the dholes looked up, its muzzle soaked in red, eyes sharp, before returning to the feast. The rest of the pack rustled unseen nearby, hidden behind the cover of the thorny undergrowth.

"That's a fresh kill," Surya whispered, a note of awe and something else, creeping into his voice.

Then, without warning, a loud trumpet split the air.

One of the cow elephants charged forward with her ears flared wide, trunk raised, feet pounding the ground as she stormed toward the bushes. The dholes didn't wait. In seconds, the visible ones abandoned the carcass and vanished into the undergrowth. The sound of snapping twigs and dry leaves followed their escape. One last dhole, caught mid-bite, grabbed a scrap of flesh and slipped away with it.

Only the hind limb remained half-eaten, blood-soaked, and twitching slightly in the breeze.

"That was incredible," Ananth whispered, his voice low and reverent. "They chased them away…"

"Elephants don't like the smell of blood or the presence of predators," Gangayya said calmly, his eyes still on the herd.

As the trumpeting faded, the elephants turned their attention elsewhere. Their trunks began to wave again, sampling the air in long, slow arcs. All four lifted their heads slightly, and in perfect unison, turned in the direction of the students.

"Keep quiet," Rishi murmured, his voice barely audible, as he lowered himself further behind the bush.

Gangayya crouched, picked up a handful of dry leaves, crushed them in his palm, and released the bits slowly. The brittle flakes floated into the breeze and drifted right and toward the elephants.

"They've caught our scent," he said softly. "The wind's carrying it to them."

The group froze.

The lead female reacted instantly. She took one step forward, eyes fixed, and gently nudged the juvenile into the center. The other two females closed ranks, placing their massive bodies between the youngster and the perceived danger. Slowly, cautiously, they began retreating. Their eyes never left the direction of the wind. Not once did they turn their backs. And then, like ghosts, they melted into the forest being silent, deliberate, and majestic.

The basin, once so alive, now felt still.

Even the birds had gone quiet.

A few minutes passed before Gangayya gestured for them to move. They rose carefully, stepping back onto the trail, hearts still beating fast from the encounter.

As they continued walking, Sukhanya pointed ahead. "Look," she said. "What's that?"

Just beyond the trees, half-hidden under a thick lantana bush, stood an old structure. Small and square, its stone walls darkened by time, the roof partially collapsed. It looked like a forgotten ruin swallowed by the forest.

They approached cautiously.

Inside, tucked in what remained of a sanctum, were several stone idols most of them were curled spectacled cobras with raised hoods, their surfaces streaked with age and smudges of old vermilion. Moss crept over the base stones, and dry leaves lay scattered across the floor.

"A shrine," Netra said softly, kneeling near the entrance and brushing away a layer of leaves with the back of her hand.

Gangayya stood at a respectful distance, his face thoughtful.

"There used to be a village here," he said quietly. "Long ago. Before this became a Tiger reserve. A small one in which only a few families. This was their shrine."

The students stood silently, imagining homes, voices, festivals, and laughter, but now all vanished into the trees.

"What happened to them?" Ananth asked.

"They were relocated," Gangayya replied. "When this area was declared a tiger reserve. It's been years now."

A breeze stirred the forest, rustling the leaves overhead.

"How many tigers are there now?" Surya asked, looking around as though he might spot one.

Gangayya paused, squinting into the distance. "Hard to say exactly. Maybe a few here. More in the deep core zones. But you won't see them unless they want to be seen. They know this forest better than anyone else."

The students stood in silence, and almost instinctively, each of them brought their fingertips to their lips, kissed them gently, and touched their foreheads. A silent gesture of reverence passed down through generations.

Though the village had vanished, its memory lived in stone, in stories, and now, in them.

"Let's go," Gangayya said gently.

And so they moved on, deeper into the forest, the shadows growing longer, the trees older, and their journey just beginning.

THE LOST SIGNAL AND A SURPRISE

The forest trail beyond the old shrine curved gently downhill, with sunlight now slicing through the higher canopy. The team moved in single file, their boots softly crunching over dry leaves and the occasional snapped twig. Rishi led with Gangayya, the rest quietly following. After the early morning trek, they were now better attuned to the sounds around them, the whistle of a distant bird, the chatter of tree crickets, the rustle of branches from a squirrel's leap.

Gangayya suddenly paused and raised a hand.

"Look there," he whispered, pointing with his stick. "You see that?" His voice was low, but his eyes were sharp.

They followed his gaze. On a patch of sunlit mud by a stream edge were clear imprints, large, rounded, and distinctly toe-marked.

"Elephant footprints?" Nethra asked, leaning forward.

"Right. This might be last night," Gangayya said. "These tiny Pad marks of a calf. Most likely the Sumangali herd. You can tell by the depth, spacing, and shape. The calf's prints are light… see?"

They crouched around the tracks, taking turns measuring, sketching, and photographing. For Sukhanya, it was a thrill to map the impressions against the guidebooks they'd studied. For Anantha, the real joy was seeing something untouched, raw and direct from the forest.

Moving ahead, they saw another pile of dung which was already disintegrated.

"Jungle fowls might have done this job to search for beetles and other insects." Said Gangayya.

A few meters ahead of the disintegrated dung pile, Nethra spotted something moving erratically near a patch of dappled sunlight.

"Hey, what's that?" she asked, crouching down.

Everyone gathered around to see a small, dark beetle which was no bigger than a two-rupee coin, pushing a perfectly round ball of dung backward with its hind legs.

"A dung beetle," said Rishi, eyes lighting up. "This is incredible."

He crouched beside it, watching the meticulous way the insect maneuvered the dung ball over small twigs and stones.

"They collect fresh dung and roll it into balls like this to use it as a brood chamber. If this one's a male, he's probably trying to impress a female. Once he rolls it far enough, he'll dig a hole, bury it, and try to get her to lay eggs inside it."

Anantha frowned, watching the beetle struggle over a bump. "That's a lot of work for something that can get stolen in seconds."

Rishi nodded. "Exactly. Other dung beetles are known to follow the scent trail and steal these balls if the original roller isn't quick or careful enough. They're called kleptoparasites, dung thieves, basically."

The beetle paused, adjusting the ball's position, then resumed pushing.

Again, after moving forward and walking several hundred meters, it was noon, the sun was warm enough for sweat to bead under their collars. They found a large tamarind tree with a flat shaded patch. Gangayya declared a break. "We'll eat here."

They all gladly sank to the ground, weary but content. Gangayya opened the two boxes he had packed, a large one filled with steaming rice and sambar, and a tiny one containing fiery cut mango pickle. Pointing toward a nearby teak plant, he instructed the five to pluck six leaves each and rinse them with the last few sips of water from their nearly empty bottles, to use as natural food plates. As they followed his instructions, Gangayya grinned and added, "Here's a trick you should know." He plucked a tender new teak leaf, small and soft, he rubbed it briskly on the back of his hand. Instantly, a deep reddish stain appeared. "Natural lipstick," he chuckled, holding out his hand for them to see. The group burst into laughter, but Rishi was already smearing some on his lips with dramatic flair, prompting hoots from the others. Even in the middle of a dusty forest, the old tracker's simple wisdom brought both knowledge and joy to the moment.

They placed all the leaves on the ground and gangayya started to serve them the food. As they started eating, a sudden rustle from above startled Anantha, who dropped a bit of pickle on his shirt. A long tail swung down, followed by a curious black face with white ruff.

A langur.

It eyed them from a lower branch, sniffing the air dramatically.

"It might be the aroma of the sambar," Surya said, grinning.

The langur sat staring at them with the patience of a monk, then slowly moved on when it was clear no food would be shared.

Just then, a crackly sound interrupted the silence. Gangayya's walkie-talkie came alive with a distorted voice.

"...zrrrrk...Gangayya...cozrrrk...camp..."

He got up, adjusting his position and walking a few steps in different directions. "Signal's weak here," he muttered, raising it higher. "Maybe if I move toward that ridge..."

He tried two more times but failed to get a clear message. "Must not be urgent," he said finally, but his brow creased slightly. He tucked the device back in and joined them again, but his senses seemed slightly alert now.

After the break, the team walked two more hours. But despite all efforts, they saw no sign of Sumangali and her calf.

"Maybe they moved toward the swamp side," Gangayya said, looking at the droppings near a bend. "Still fresh, but no visual."

There was a tinge of disappointment in the team. They had hoped to see the famous herd with a newborn.

By 4:00 PM, they reached the coconut grove, tired, dusty, and satisfied. The sun had mellowed into a soft orange hue. The jeep was parked at the edge, slightly tilted, and Baala was inside, arms folded, snoring lightly.

Gangayya chuckled. "Our chariot awaits."

Surya tapped the hood gently. "Wake up, driver-sir. We have returned."

Baala blinked awake, yawned like a lion, and asked, "Saw anything?"

"No Sumangali, but a different herd and a pack of dholes" said Rishi.

"Not bad for day one," Baala said, grinning as he started the jeep.

They reached the camp around 4:30 PM, and as the vehicle slowed past the kitchen shed, Nethra was the first to spot the figure standing near the elephant feeding area.

“Wait, is that…?”

“IBRAHIM?” Anantha shouted.

Sure enough, the familiar frame of Ibrahim stood, grinning sheepishly. A forest guard near him waved at the team and said, “Tried to reach you on walkie, but no signal. The ACF dropped him off. Said he’ll stay with your team for a few days.”

“You made it!” said Surya, clapping him on the back.

Before Ibrahim could explain more, Gangayya appeared and said, “It’s feeding time now. Want to come?”

“Of course!” they all said in chorus.

They washed hands and feet at the tap and followed Gangayya into the elephant kitchen. The earthy smell of jaggery and ragi filled the air. Staff members were rolling massive balls of food, football-sized ragi-laden bundles.

The students helped for a while, carefully pressing the mixture and handing it over to the mahouts. Just then, they noticed Veera’s mahout and kavadi heading toward the back enclosure with a tray full of ragi balls.

“He’s going to Veera,” Rishi whispered. “Let’s follow.”

They walked quietly, and soon saw Veera, majestic even in the fading light. But just as they approached, he shifted, turned away from them, and calmly began scratching himself.

His massive penis was fully out and touched the ground. The elephant lifted his left hind limb and started rubbing it gently against his penis to relieve an itch.

Ibrahim stared, stunned. "Wait… where are his nuts? Are elephants neutered or something?"

The others laughed, and Rishi shook his head. "No, no. Elephants have internal testicles, unlike most mammals. They're inside, near the kidneys."

In elephants, the testes are located intra-abdominally, rather than in a scrotal sac as seen in many other mammalian species. This retention of testicles within the body cavity is hypothesized to be an evolutionary adaptation linked to their large body size, low sperm competition, and thermoregulatory constraints. Unlike species with external testes, where spermatogenesis requires a cooler temperature and elephants maintain testicular function at core body temperatures, suggesting the presence of physiological mechanisms that enable efficient sperm production without the need for external cooling. Additionally, the absence of a scrotum reduces the risk of injury or parasitism in dense vegetation and during intraspecific conflicts, particularly during musth.

"Oh," said Ibrahim, clearly fascinated. "So he's not… neutered?"

"Nope. In fact, Veera is the father of the calf we're here to study."

"WHAT?"

Before Ibrahim could recover, the mahout turned to them. "Do you want to feed him? Don't worry, I'm right here."

One by one, the students took turns holding out broken food balls. Veera accepted them calmly, his trunk moving with precision, touching each person briefly before placing the bundle into his mouth.

The sky behind him turned a deep purple, scattered with streaks of orange.

By the time they finished, the camp lights were flickering on. Everyone headed to their quarters, changed into fresher clothes, and stepped out again, where a group of mahouts had lit a fire for warmth and to ward off mosquitoes. Laughter and murmured conversation drifted through the night air.

Gangayya saw the students lingering nearby and realized they might hesitate to join the larger group.

He quietly set up a smaller fire for them just outside their quarters. "Sit here. A tracker will bring your food today. Eat and rest. Tomorrow, we start at 10 AM. A vet from Bengaluru is coming and I have to assist with a treatment. You can join us if you'd like."

They all nodded eagerly.

As they settled around the flames, Ibrahim sat cross-legged, eyes gleaming with questions. "So… tell me everything. What did I miss today?"

The stories poured out, every track, every call, every missed signal, and every sweaty, unforgettable moment.

Ibrahim listened, half-jealous, half-thrilled.

"Don't worry," Rishi told him finally, noticing his long face. "We've only just begun. The best field days are still ahead."

The fire crackled between them, casting long shadows. Around them, the forest settled into its night rhythm and the team, now complete, felt more ready than ever.

SCRUBS AND SCIENCE

The morning air was sharp, cutting through the fabric of their clothes as the team stirred early from their beds. At 8:30 AM, each of them clutched their favorite jaggery tea, steam curling up like wisps from the forest floor. By 9:15, breakfast had been served. It was neeruppittu, a watery pudding delicately flavored with chilli and coconut. They licked their plates clean, washed them, and returned them to the kitchen with content smiles.

Wandering across the camp, aimless and full, the six of them roamed between enclosures, the kitchen, and the watchtower. Suddenly, a loud voice rang out across the compound.

"Oye! Do you want to join me to scrub Veera? It's bath time!"

It was Veera's mahout. The group exchanged excited glances and rushed over to join him. They walked with him down the well-trodden path to the pond, where Veera, the majestic tusker, was already stepping slowly into the water. With a gentle groan, he half-lay sideways into the pond, one side of his body submerged.

The mahout quickly climbed up onto Veera's exposed hip and shouted, "Come on! Get in here! Grab these!"

He handed them each a rough coil of coconut husk rope.

"Splash water first, then scrub hard! The dirt has to go."

The team entered the pond one by one, calf-deep, getting used to the chill. Rishi made his way toward Veera's head, curious about the thick, viscous secretion from his temporal gland area.

"He might be in post-musth now," he said, dipping his fingers in the thick fluid. He sniffed it. No unusual odor.

Musth can be delineated into three distinct physiological and behavioral phases: early-musth, full musth, and post-musth. During the pre-musth phase, individuals exhibit mild signs such as temporal gland swelling, occasional urine dribbling, and increased restlessness, often accompanied by a rise in circulating androgens, particularly testosterone. This phase serves as a preparatory period for the hormonal surge and social changes to follow. The peak musth phase is characterized by pronounced temporal gland secretion, continuous urine dribbling, elevated testosterone levels, heightened aggression, reduced feeding, and intense mate-seeking behavior. Bulls in peak musth may become highly intolerant of other males and display increased dominance in social hierarchies. In the post-musth phase, physiological parameters gradually return to baseline; behavioral aggression subsides, temporal secretions cease, and the animal resumes normal feeding and social interactions. These phases represent a hormonally regulated cycle that plays a critical role in the reproductive strategy and social dynamics of adult male elephants.

With Veera relaxed in the water, they scrubbed vigorously, down his flanks, under his belly, over his massive feet. The rope scraped off a day's worth of caked mud and dry skin.

After nearly an hour and a half, the mahout brought a handful of coarse sand and began scrubbing Veera's tusks from the tips right up to the gum line.

Rishi, curious again, asked, "Why clean so deep into the tusk base?"

The mahout called them close. "Look here," he said, gently lifting the flap of skin near Veera's right tusk. "See those?"

Tiny white capsules, no bigger than grains of rice, were tucked near the base.

"Fly eggs," he said. "Some flies lay here. If not cleaned, they hatch. The maggots burrow and rot the tusk base. That's how tusks decay. Looks small now, but the risk is big."

Ibrahim frowned. "But what about wild elephants? Who cleans theirs?"

The mahout grinned. "Good question. In the wild, they find tree trunks and rocky outcrops. They rub themselves, especially their tusks against rough bark. You'll often see elephants standing near certain trees, shifting their heads side to side. That's how they remove dirt. It's instinct. But here, we become the bark."

The team fell silent, surprised, not just by the biology, but by how deeply the mahout understood it.

Soon after that, Veera rose from the pond and followed his mahout back to his enclosure. The students, now drenched, asked Gangayya about the vet and the day's plan.

"I don't know what's delaying her," he replied. "Once she's done with treatment, we'll go to the field. No walking today. We'll do a jeep drive to three water bodies I've seen the herd frequent."

Ibrahim looked relieved.

The others? Disappointed. The long walks were their windows into learning the signs, dung, calls, the rhythm of the forest underfoot.

Before the discussion could go further, a jeep engine echoed through the camp. A white vehicle pulled into the compound. Everyone turned.

Dr. Nikita had arrived.

She stepped out, tying her hair into a bun, wearing a khaki shirt and a field kit slung across her shoulder. The guards and trackers, including Gangayya, immediately approached her and saluted. She returned each greeting with equal respect.

"Madam, this is the student team," said Gangayya, introducing them.

She smiled warmly. "So you're the ones here for the calf study. That's excellent."

Before they could speak more, she turned toward the elephant enclosure.

"Let's attend to Sundra first," she said.

Sundra was a 60-year-old bull, still imposing, with medium-length tusks and wise, sunken eyes. His mahout pointed to a wound on his right thigh, which was deep, inflamed, likely the result of a tusk jab during a recent wild elephant capture mission.

Rishi's eyes widened. "That must've been the one in the kraal."

Dr. Nikita cleaned the wound with antiseptic, flushed it with saline. She applied a dark coloured paste and handed over the leftover box of paste to the mahout asking him to regularly apply it.

"Give him these antibiotics daily for five days," she told the mahout, handing over a pouch. "And monitor the wound for any discharge or swelling."

The students huddled nearby, whispering observations.

Later, as the tea was served, Dr. Nikita removed her gloves, washed up, and joined them briefly.

Sukhanya leaned forward. "Madam, if you don't mind, what's your background?"

The vet smiled. "Masters in Veterinary Science, wildlife specialization. With great difficulty, I gained an opportunity to work with elephants and rhinos in Africa and that's what gained me a job here."

"But why come back from Africa?" asked Anantha.

"I have worked for two years there and I think that's enough. I want to serve my country too," said Dr. Nikita.

Just then, Baala announced, "Lunch is ready."

To everyone's surprise, Dr. Nikita joined them for lunch.

Lunch was ragi balls and spinach sambar. As the team began eating, Dr. Nikita continued her conversation.

"If you're studying elephants and their herds, try to record both direct and indirect signs," she said between bites. "Droppings, footprints, vocalizations, bark scrapings, broken branches, all these helps build context."

"Yes ma'am, gangayya has been guiding us with all these," said Rishi.

"He is a walking institution," she replied. "There's plenty for us to learn from him."

Everyone listened closely, eating slower than usual, absorbing every word.

She sipped her buttermilk and smiled, "Also, make sure you document weather patterns, it all affects movement."

The team nodded, scribbling notes even during the meal.

As she stood up, brushing off her hands, she said warmly, "You're on the right path. Just keep your eyes open. Sometimes the most important data is what you don't expect."

"And remember, zoologists and wildlife biologists like you are just as crucial as vets. Conservation isn't a one-person job. It's a field of collaboration." She added.

With a final wave, she climbed into the jeep and left for her meeting at Mysuru Zoo.

Baala and Gangayya returned. "Let's eat quickly," said Gangayya. "We leave in 30 minutes."

Soon, they were packed into the jeep, heading out.

"Three water bodies," said Gangayya, "and if time permits, a farmer who last saw the herd. Good chance for some data."

"Fringe data's critical," said Sukhanya, already flipping pages. "We need to make a separate entry sheet for farmer reports."

Rishi pulled out a fresh notebook and started a column titled *Fringe Sightings and Human Sources.*

About 20 minutes into the drive, Baala slowed the vehicle.

"Why are we stopping?" asked Nethra.

"Look left," said Baala, pointing into a thicket of bamboo.

A massive black figure stood still, a 6 feet tall at the shoulder.

"A male gaur," said Gangayya. "Shining coat, broad horns. This one can take down a leopard."

They watched silently as the beast stared back, then faded into the undergrowth.

After another 10-minute drive, they reached the first water body.

It was looking beautiful with the flowering water hyacinth but it was choking the water body. A male sambar deer, alert and proud, stood at the water's edge. He suddenly barked, making a loud, guttural sound and stomped his feet.

"Alarm call," Rishi whispered. "They do that when they smell a predator or hear unfamiliar movement."

Baala, quietly listening, nodded. "That sambar knows more than we do."

The sambar vanished seconds later into the lantana bushes.

The team got down, walked slowly toward the edge, then noticed a dung pile about 100 meters away.

They moved toward it. It was dry and from the center of the dung, three tiny saplings had emerged, each about 4 inches tall.

The low digestion efficiency, not only influences their foraging ecology, necessitating the consumption of large volumes of vegetation daily. It also renders elephant dung a valuable resource for ecological processes such as seed dispersal and nutrient cycling.

"Is this seed dispersal?" Ibrahim asked.

"Yes," said Sukhanya and Gangayya in unison. "Elephants are the engineers of the forest."

They began digging through another dung pile which was older, dry, no plants yet. Scribbled notes. Cross-checks. Nothing extraordinary.

"We might not see them today either," sighed Surya.

"Not always easy," Gangayya said. "But you're already lucky. A herd chasing dholes? That's a story in itself."

He raised a hand, signaling the team to move on.

"Let's go slow. Stay sharp. The forest always has more to show."

THE BROKEN TRENCH

The jeep rolled slowly from the first water body, where the only thrill had been the barking sambar deer and a seedling-laced dung pile. The second water body, about fifteen minutes away, was nestled between a curve of acacia trees, abandoned and bleached by the sun.

Baala cut the engine. "Let's be quick. Not much shade here."

The team climbed down one by one, shoes crunching the dry leaf litter. The water body was half full, lined with marsh grasses. Gangayya scanned the bank, motioning the team to split up and flank the perimeter.

But the signs were clear, no fresh dung, no broken branches, not even a disturbed patch of grass. Just a few langurs who chattered from the trees, warning their kin about the intruders.

"Nothing here either," sighed Surya.

Still, they decided to wait for a while, hoping for some wildlife moment to unfold. The sun was high but tolerable under the slight breeze rustling through the trees.

Then Gangayya turned to the group, a playful glint in his eye. "Have you seen crabs before? Tasted them?"

Ibrahim looked intrigued. "Crabs? In a water body like this?"

"Wait, let me show you," Gangayya said, walking toward a huge rock that jutted halfway into the water and halfway onto the muddy bank. He folded his pants up to the knees and stepped carefully into the muck, positioning himself beside the rock.

With practiced ease, he slid his hands beneath the rock's edge, feeling his way along the cool stone.

Suddenly, he yelped. "Ahhh! This one got hold of my thumb."

He lifted his hand out of the water, a medium-sized dark-colored crab clinging stubbornly to his finger.

"If you all weren't here," Gangayya said with a grin, gently detaching the crab and letting it drop back, "this guy would've made it to camp for dinner. But not today. No hunting when you're around."

Back into the jeep. Dust puffed up from the wheels as Baala guided them toward the third water body, this one deeper, shaded, and ringed with large stones. As they neared, something moved.

"There!" shouted Nethra.

Everyone shook for a minutes, thinking it was an elephant.

"On the rock, the middle one" added Nethra.

A large marsh crocodile was basking lazily on a sunlit rock, its grey body gleaming faintly. But the moment the jeep neared, it slid soundlessly into the water.

By the time the team had climbed down and approached the edge of the pool, all they could see was its knobby snout and glassy eyes, floating like a half-submerged ghost.

"Only the head's visible now," whispered Rishi.

"Marsh crocodile," Gangayya confirmed. "And a big one. Could be ten feet."

They noted down the sighting and surveyed the bankline. No elephant activity. No tracks. Just the distant call of a black kite and the ripple of water from the crocodile.

It was only 4 PM and still bright, so Gangayya made a quick decision.

"Let's go meet Manjunatha, the farmer who last saw the herd."

Ibrahim sat upright. "Finally, a human source!"

Within twenty minutes, they were passing through narrow dirt roads, flanked by patches of paddy swaying gently in the wind. They reached a humble house beside a green stretch of farmland, where an elderly man was checking his field bunds.

Gangayya waved. "Manjunatha, avare! These are the students from Mysuru."

Manjunatha wiped his hands on his dhoti and nodded at the group. "Welcome. You've come for the elephants?"

He led them to a shaded patch under a mango tree and sat cross-legged.

"They came four nights ago," he began. "Seven of them, they were all big without tusks. And one tiny calf stuck close to one elephant's belly. I couldn't tell if it was the mother. Which But they were agitated. Tails up, heads raised. No sound, but their eyes... like fire."

He looked toward the paddy field, voice tightening. "They stampeded through it, took them less than ten mintues to flatten everything."

Rishi asked, "Did they enter from the trench side?"

"Yes, the broken section near the tamarind tree."

"Did they make any sounds?" Nethra asked.

"No," Manjunatha shook his head. "They were silent... but angry. Even the calf looked scared."

Sukhanya leaned forward, "Did they feed on anything?

"They used to come near my house during jackfruit season. But not now. Ever since the calf came, they avoid coming close. They just cross the field to get to the other side of the forest."

"What about the herd's movement?" asked Surya. "Any patterns?"

"They used to come once a month. Now it's almost a week from the last time I've seen them. That trench doesn't stop them anymore. But I've seen this herd for months now. The calf is a new addition. Their behavior has changed since then, more cautious, more aggressive."

Just then, a middle-aged woman walked over with a tray of steel tumblers. "Here, have some tea," she smiled. "You all look tired."

Gangayya stood up. "This is Pallavi, Manjunatha's wife."

The students greeted her warmly. "Thank you, madam," said Anantha.

As they sipped the hot tea, Sukhanya continued questioning. "Have you seen calves before?"

Manjunatha scratched his chin. "Yes, but not like this one. It was too jumpy. Not like the others I've seen years ago, which played and lagged behind. This one stuck like glue to the adult."

Rishi noted the time, direction, calf behavior, damage done, and possible entry and exit points.

"What kind of damage did they do before?" asked Ibrahim.

Pallavi stepped forward. "About a month ago, they broke the water pipes and fencing. We spent 7,000 rupees to fix it. Applied for compensation, but no word from the department yet."

Gangayya looked down, his expression tightening.

"But unlike other farmers," Manjunatha added gently, "we know elephants belong to the forest. We don't want to hurt them. Some here talk of electric fences with direct current. We don't support that."

The team glanced at each other, humbled. To hear compassion from a family that had suffered losses was rare.

"Other animals?" asked Ibrahim.

"chukke jinke (spotted deer), wild boars and peafowls. They eat and ruin the crops too."

"We'll return soon for more, got plenty of work to finish before the night " said Gangayya gently. "Thanks for your time."

The team thanked Pallavi again and walked back to the jeep, data sheets fuller than before. The air began to cool. Faint mist rolled in from the eastern edge of the forest.

Back at camp, they freshened up quickly, changed into dry clothes, and spread their notebooks and data sheets across the cemented floor. Their first day of data collection which was modest, but meaningful.

Dung notes, tracker interviews, field signs, and the interview with Manjunatha… everything was organized and discussed. The energy in the room was buzzing.

Then came Gangayya, hands on hips, a slight grin on his face.

"I have duty tonight," he said. "Near the broken trench. Someone has to guard it. Want to join?"

He paused. "There's a tree hut, an old tamarind tree. Good view of the trench. Elephants might cross tonight. No guarantees, but if you're lucky... you'll see them. At midnight."

Ibrahim's eyes lit up. "Tree hut? Midnight watch? I'm in!"

"Don't get too excited," said Baala from behind. "Mosquitoes, flying foxes, and god knows what else."

Surya added, "We'll pull up the ladder once we climb. No way a sloth bear's climbing up on us."

They agreed.

After a dinner of hot ragi rotis, brinjal curry, and curd, they packed some torches, notebooks, and insect repellent. Baala drove them to the base of the old tamarind tree, which stood tall like a silent sentinel near the broken trench.

A rickety bamboo ladder leaned against the bark. Gangayya lit a small fire and handed them an old sickle. "Just in case."

One by one, they climbed into the wooden platform nestled in the branches. The view was perfect. The trench below stretched like a shadowed line through the jungle.

Owls called.

And far in the distance… a soft rumble.

Rishi leaned forward. "Did you hear that?"

Everyone froze. Somewhere in the dark, a branch cracked.

The night had just begun.

FINALLY!! SUMANGALI!!

The wooden platform creaked as the team shifted their weight, trying to find comfortable positions. The tree hut, built snugly in the crook of the tamarind tree, offered a wide view of the broken trench below. A pale moon floated above the forest, bathing the land in an eerie silver sheen. Below, the small fire crackled gently, throwing flickering shadows across the ground.

For the first hour, it was just them and the sounds of the nightjars, and the distant, booming call of a jungle owl. Gangayya sat near the edge, scanning with his sharp eyes, while the rest whispered among themselves.

"My spine's giving up," grumbled Surya.

"Try sitting cross-legged," suggested Sukhanya, munching on a dry biscuit. "You'll forget your back pain and just lose all feeling in your legs instead."

Ibrahim had his notebook open, scribbling a journal entry by torchlight. "If we actually see elephants tonight, this will go into the top five days of my life."

Anantha leaned over the edge. "What if they cross through the broken trench while we're half asleep?"

"Don't worry," Gangayya said, eyes fixed. "They'll announce themselves. You'll feel the vibration before you see them."

Time passed slowly. Almost three hours into the night, the wind shifted slightly. Gangayya suddenly raised a hand.

"Quiet."

The team froze. In the distance, a rhythmic thud began, soft at first, then unmistakable.

Thump… thump… crunch…

Branches cracked. The bamboo behind the trench rustled.

"Look there," whispered Rishi, pointing through the leaves.

A silhouette appeared, massive, slow-moving, almost spectral in the moonlight. Then another. And another.

"It's an elephant herd," Gangayya confirmed, voice low. "They're approaching the trench. Quickly grab the crackers. We have to make a disturbing sound and send them back into the forest, or else they're going to cross."

He lit two noise crackers and flung them into the air, away from the herd. The explosions echoed through the forest. The elephants flinched but kept moving steadily, unfazed.

Gangayya tried again with two more, then the last of the six. But the herd pushed on, slow and focused, as if they'd dealt with these distractions before. The trench guarding attempt had failed.

But something extraordinary was unfolding.

From the tree hut, they watched as the elephants moved in a tight cluster. One larger female paused, sniffed the air. No calf was seen initially, but then, a tiny trunk peeked out from beneath one elephant's belly.

"It's a calf!" Nethra whispered with excitement.

"Yes… that's Sumangali, the mother," said Gangayya. Sukhanya almost had tears in her eyes.

The matriarch stopped at the trench, inspecting the shallow gap. She turned sideways and let out a low rumble. The others followed her lead, but the calf hesitated, unable to cross the drop.

Sumangali, clearly distressed, stepped into the trench. She tried nudging the calf up, but it only managed a few steps before slipping back.

Then, the biggest female stepped in. She bent her knees, lowering her enormous body into a squat. Curling her trunk, she scooped under the calf's belly and, with great effort, dragged it gently onto the bank.

The entire team sat motionless, their breath caught in awe. The intelligence, coordination and the maternal care.

It was beyond words.

Suddenly, a loud trumpet broke the silence, not a warning, but a cry of frustration.

"They've sensed us," whispered Gangayya. "Don't move. No lights."

The herd hesitated and the forest itself seemed to pause.

Then the matriarch gave a low grunt. One by one, the elephants veered off, not back into the forest but alongside the trench, moving in a parallel line through the shadows.

"Did they turn back?" asked Anantha.

"No," Gangayya murmured. "They're finding another way."

They waited, tense and wide-eyed. But the herd didn't return.

By 5 AM, fatigue settled in. Ibrahim had dozed off, head resting on his backpack. Nethra, ever hopeful, was still peeking out through the side slit of the hut, pencil in hand, sketching what she could remember.

As dawn painted the sky a muted orange, the forest stirred once more. Parakeets screeched, langurs chattered in the treetops, and somewhere distant, a sambar deer called out.

They climbed down the ladder, one by one, careful and quiet. Gangayya poured soil over the fire, smothering the last embers.

The team then walked quietly toward the broken trench. The earth was soft from the early dew. They spread out, eyes scanning for footprints, drag marks, and dung.

"Look here," said Surya, pointing to a perfect pad mark which was round, crisp, with toe imprints clearly visible.

Sukhanya quickly took out the measuring tape. "This one's about twenty-one centimeters."

"Check the stride length," said Rishi, moving along the trail.

They began taking measurements, widths, depths, distances between pads, and even the trench itself. Ibrahim noted, "The trench is only about 2 feet at this spot."

Nethra was sketching the trench profile while Anantha used a stick to check the softness of the bottom where the calf had slipped.

It wasn't just observation, it was analysis too. The height of the calf was estimated against the side of the trench where the mother had stood. Broken twigs, dragged soil, the arc of movement and it was all coming together.

Back at camp, they freshened up, bleary-eyed but glowing.

"We saw the herd," Rishi said, half in disbelief.

"And the calf," added Surya. "Right in front of us."

Sukhanya flipped open her field diary. "Let's document everything. Time, behavior, trench interaction, that lifting moment…"

They spent the next hour logging their observations. Detailed, structured and careful. It was their most unforgettable night.

Gangayya watched them, pride in his eyes. "Now you're doing the real field work."

THE FAKE FOREST

After breakfast, they retreated to their room, closed the doors, and let their bodies rest. Ibrahim collapsed on the floor mat with a muffled grunt, while Surya curled near the window, the open notebook still tucked under his arm. The silence stretched into late morning, broken only by the whir of the fan and an occasional snore.

By afternoon, they were gathered again, notebooks open, measuring tapes on the table, field sketches scattered across the floor.

"Let's start logging the data," Nethra said, pulling up her notes. "Time of herd arrival was approximately 2:13 AM."

"Trench depth, only just 3 feet where the calf tried to cross," said Rishi. "It clearly wasn't enough."

They began charting the herd's movement. Using the broken twigs, footprints, and drag marks, they reconstructed the sequence.

"Now," said Anantha, flipping through farmer Manjayya's past reports. "Here, before the calf was born, Sumangali's herd visited his farm maybe once a month.

"That's a pattern," said Surya. "But now the calf has changed the herd's dynamics. Maybe it's about feeding or protection."

Just then, there was a knock on the door.

Baala's voice called out, "Ayyo, one of your man has arrived. Scientist Pranay sir is at the camp."

The team jumped up like they had fresh batteries in them.

Moments later, under the thatched roof of the dining area, they greeted Mr. Pranay. He welcomed them with a quiet nod and sat cross-legged on the bench.

They began explaining the night's events over early lunch. The trench crossing, the behavior of the herd, the calf's hesitation, Sumangali's actions and everything.

He listened intently, pausing only to ask for time stamps and trench dimensions.

"And the fire crackers?" he asked.

"Used. Six of them. Didn't work," said Gangayya. "The herd knew what they were. It's like they didn't care."

Pranay gave a thoughtful nod.

An hour later, they all piled into the jeep, the team, Pranay, Gangayya and Baala. Their destination the path the herd had taken after crossing the trench.

The forest road was damp and muddy from last week's rain. Not long into the drive, Gangayya signaled to stop. Fresh pad marks.

The team jumped down. There was a pile of dung nearby, fresh and steaming slightly in the midday heat.

Pranay knelt beside it. "This is less than 10 hours old. Notice the fiber content," he pointed. "Looks like they've fed on coarse crops, possibly sugarcane."

As they continued, the jeep reached a patch of land that didn't quite look like forest, but it wasn't farmland either.

"This looks… abandoned," said Nethra.

Gangayya nodded. "This belongs to a farmer named Rajashekar. He moved to Bengaluru five years ago. His son got a job there. No one farms here anymore."

The area was dense with overgrowth. Tall grasses, wild shrubs, and a scattering of young rain trees.

"Look," said Surya, pointing to a broken branch. A clear trail had been made through the foliage.

"They've been using this often," murmured Pranay. "But there's not much edible vegetation here. Not their usual feed."

They moved ahead. Suddenly, a commotion came into view.

A small group of villagers stood clustered with a few uniformed forest staff. The team approached. A one-acre sugarcane field had been flattened, stalks trampled, leaves shredded.

A tired-looking farmer was speaking animatedly to the officer. "Three in the morning. I heard the rustling but didn't come out. By dawn, everything was gone. All my work, gone in a night."

While the department staff recorded the case, the team got to work. Rishi and Anantha measured the extent of the damage, sukhanya recorded plant density, nethra sketched and Ibrahim spoke to the farmer.

"How often does this happen?" he asked.

"Rarely. Maybe once in a year," the farmer replied. "But now... I've lost everything. This was my best patch."

Gangayya and Pranay exchanged glances. "Sumangali's herd again," said Pranay softly.

Back in the jeep, as they drove away, Pranay seemed deep in thought. Then he tapped Baala on the shoulder.

"Let's go back to that abandoned land."

He also told Ibrahim to measure the distance from here to the abandoned land.

Ibrahim pulled out the GPS and once there, “Four kilometers, sir.” He said.

“Good,” said Pranay. “Now, from this spot to the broken trench?”

“Approximately 980 meters,” reported Anantha looking at his notes.

The scientist turned slowly, gazing at the narrow corridor through the overgrowth.

“It’s brilliant,” he said. “They’re using this patch as a cover. The trench crossing happens around 2 AM. Within few minutes, they’re in this overgrown land. It looks like forest, so no one notices, no barking dogs, no torchlights. They rest here, regroup maybe. And they quietly reach the electric pole, from which it’s just 350 meters to the sugarcane field.”

He drew a rough map on the soil with a stick.

“From forest to trench… trench to this abandoned land… and then to the crop field. That’s the route.”

The team stared at the forgotten land, a place that once fed humans, now offering an unnecessary passage to wild giants.

“Sometimes,” Pranay said softly, “elephants don’t just remember paths. They innovate. And when we fail to keep up with their memory… they find newer ways.”

The sun dipped low as they stood in the middle of that forgotten land, a place that once fed humans, now offering an unnecessary passage to wild giants.

Now, near the broken trench, pranay stepped out quietly, surveying the trench. "Measure the length of the break," he murmured, half to himself. "It looks small, thankfully."

Anantha and Rishi moved with the tape. "Four meters exactly," Rishi called.

"Four meters," Pranay echoed. "That's all it takes."

The trench wasn't just broken, it had begun to vanish. Weeds and vines had grown inside it, softening its edge. It no longer looked like a barrier, but a natural dip in the earth.

"That's how they came through in a line," said Nethra. "One by one."

"There were places," Gangayya added, "where the trench was broken for 100 meters or more. The whole herd walks through shoulder to shoulder. But this one's small. Still…"

"When can it be repaired?" asked Pranay, scanning the vegetation.

Gangayya snorted, frustrated. "We told the higher officers a month ago. No one's moved. Meanwhile, we keep watch all night from tree huts. No sleep, no support."

Everyone fell silent with no expressions and just fatigue.

They climbed back into the jeep and rolled deeper into the forest, trying to spot signs of the herd.

About twenty minutes in, Gangayya asked Baala to slow down. "Stop here," he said, pointing toward a narrow trail off the side.

They all stepped out and took a short walk through the underbrush. It was quiet, the forest alive only with the distant calls of mynas and the crunch of dry twigs underfoot. Then Nethra pointed at something small near a patch of sunlight.

"Look at that!" she said.

Two tiny mango saplings stood next to each other, their fresh leaves gleaming bright green.

Pranay looked at Gangayya with a curious expression, silently asking the question.

Before anyone could speak, Gangayya chuckled and said, "Sloth bear scat."

"What?" Ibrahim blinked.

"Bear stole mangoes from a nearby farm. Ate them whole and has done his business here. The last time I saw this, it was just a dry scat, but now, the seeds are growing into plants."

The team stared, intrigued. Ibrahim squinted at the saplings and then made a face.

"I mean, just thinking… what would it have taken for the bear to… you know… squeeze these seeds out of its back hole?"

They burst into laughter. Even Pranay smiled.

Still chuckling, they returned to the jeep.

Pranay, sitting between Sukhanya and Ibrahim, flipped through the data sheets.

"Hmmm… this is too unfiltered," he said, scribbling notes. "You've written down everything. But when you're with a wild herd, it's not practical to note so much and filter later. You'll miss critical moments."

"So…?" Surya asked, half-knowing the answer.

"We restart," Pranay said, smiling gently. "I'll help. Let's make a better format, the one that lets you tick or untick observations as they happen."

The students groaned softly, exchanging tired glances. But the disappointment was mild. The joy of being mentored directly by their scientist outweighed the task of starting over.

"It'll be easier in the long run," Mr. Pranay assured them. "When we're back at camp, we'll draft a proper template. You'll be more efficient in the field. I promise."

It was already 4 PM when they returned to the forest quarters. Pranay had to leave for Mysuru before dark.

Without wasting time, they spread the old sheets out and sat around the table as Mr. Pranay, pen in hand, began writing.

"These are the things you can observe," he said. "In both the core forest and fringe areas."

1. **GPS Coordinates**
   Accurate location of observation using handheld GPS unit.
2. **Zone Classification**
   Categorize the observation site as one of the following:
   - Core Forest Area
   - Fringe/Edge Zone
   - Outside Forest Boundary
3. **Distance to Nearest Forest Boundary (in meters)**
   Estimate or measure the distance from the observation point to the nearest forest edge or anthropogenic boundary.
4. **Calf Position within the Herd During Movement**
   Describe whether the calf is positioned at the front, middle, rear, or flanking the herd while in active motion.
5. **Calf Position within the Herd While Stationary**
   Note the calf's relative position when the herd is resting, feeding or not moving forward.
6. **Calf Interaction with Non-maternal Individuals**
   Document any observed social behaviors involving the calf and elephants other than its mother.

7. **Maximum Observed Distance of Calf from the Herd (in meters)**
   Record the farthest distance the calf strayed from the herd during the observation period.
8. **Frequency of Suckling**
   Count and note how many times suckling behavior was observed during the session.
9. **Additional Notes**
   Include any contextual details such as environmental cues, unusual behavior, presence of other species, or disturbances.

"With this," he said, "you'll have a strong base dataset. After few months, you'll have enough to expand into behavioral trends, spatial mapping, and more."

They were still copying the list when their favorite jaggery tea had come. Sipping it slowly, Pranay turned to Gangayya. "Before I leave, can I see Veera?"

Gangayya smiled. "Of course."

The entire team followed.

At the camp's far end, Veera stood like a quiet guardian, majestic, still, his tusks glinting softly in the afternoon sun.

Veera flapped his ears and gave a soft rumble when he saw them.

"I think he remembers you," said Gangayya to Pranay.

"I'm not so sure," Pranay chuckled. "But he always made me feel like he did."

They watched Veera for a while in silence, each lost in their own thoughts. Pranay stepped a little closer and whispered something under his breath, a message, a memory, or just a thank you. No one asked.

As the sun began to dip behind the trees, casting golden shadows over the forest, the team returned to the quarters.

Mr. Pranay packed lightly and turned to the students.

"You all have something special here," he said. "You've seen more than most students ever do. Don't let the paperwork bury the wild."

With a firm handshake and a warm smile, he climbed into the jeep and left for Mysuru.

The students lingered a little longer outside. The sky was glowing orange, birds flitting across it like brush strokes on a canvas.

Inside, the table was still covered in sheets, pens, and scribbled categories.

They sat down again, quietly, seriously and began building their new data sheet, as the sun set behind them and the forest prepared for another long, mysterious night.

FULL FIGURES AND AN EMERGENCY

Soon after dinner, Rishi wiped his mouth with his shirt and turned to Gangayya, a hopeful twinkle in his eye.

"Can we spend the night at the tree house again? Just a try to spot the herd again?"

Gangayya looked at the group, faces still sun-kissed from the day's work, eyes filled with that familiar mix of exhaustion and excitement. He gave a slow nod. "Alright, but only if you all promise not to doze off this time."

After wrapping up their lunch and clearing their plates, the team wasted no time. They prepped quickly, packing essentials, field books, water bottles and jackets. Baala pulled the jeep to the edge of the tamarind tree once more. The students jumped off with practiced ease.

Gangayya stayed behind for a moment to light a small fire at the base of the tree to deter any wandering wildlife. The comforting scent of smoke drifted upward as the team ascended the wooden ladder into their temporary perch above the forest.

They arranged their sleeping mats and notebooks around them. The forest seemed unusually quiet. The occasional call of a nightjar filled the air, but the broken trench below remained still.

Rishi kept his eyes locked on the trail through the leaves. Sukhanya flipped through her field notes by torchlight.

They waited until 3 AM, eyes burning with fatigue. No sign of movement, no shadow passing through the trench.

Disappointed but not disheartened, they rolled themselves into their sleeping bags and let sleep take over.

By 6:30 AM, the forest was already bathed in gold. Birds had begun their morning chorus. Rishi was the first to stir. He yawned, rubbed his eyes, and lazily peeked through the branches.

Then he froze.

"Wake up, guys… wake up! Dholes! It's a pack of dholes!"

Ibrahim was the first to sit up. "What? Where?"

The rest of the team scrambled to the side slit of the tree house.

Seven rust-colored wild dogs trotted in a perfectly spaced line, tails held confidently high. Their gait was smooth, synchronized, and fearless.

Listening to the whispers and excitement above them, the dholes paused. As one, they turned their heads and looked up at the humans curiously. Their yellow eyes shone briefly in the morning sun, and then, just as calmly, they turned and vanished into the thickets.

"No fear," Surya whispered. "They just… looked at us and left."

Once the pack had vanished from view, the team climbed down the ladder with new energy. Nethra crouched low to inspect the pug marks in the soft soil. "Perfect," he said. "Still fresh."

"Second mammal near the trench," Nethra noted, documenting the date and time. "First the elephants, now the dholes. This broken trench is definitely a problem."

They packed their bags and started walking back towards the camp. Baala, who was supposed to pick them up, was nowhere in sight.

"Guess he overslept," Rishi muttered, adjusting his bag.

Ten minutes into their walk, the familiar hum of the jeep engine cut through the quiet. Around the bend came Baala, waving sheepishly.

"Sorry sorry!" he laughed.

The students laughed too and piled into the jeep.

Back at camp, they washed up and sat at the dining shed. The aroma of jaggery tea floated around, but their stomachs grumbled for something more.

Just then, Gangayya appeared. "I need to go to the range office. Want to come?"

"Only if we eat outside," said Rishi.

Baala grinned. "There's a place I know. Doesn't look grand, but the taste… unbeatable."

Their jeep rattled along the muddy forest road. A thin mist still hung in the lower bends. They reached a roadside building with rusted iron gates, faded signboards, and the smell of pure nostalgia.

It was packed.

People stood under old ceiling fans, scooping food off banana leaves and steel plates. The kitchen clanged with activity. Steam rose in heavy clouds.

Gangayya, in his camouflage uniform, walked through the crowd like a general. No one stopped him, the students and Baala followed.

It wasn't a place to sit and eat. There were no chairs, just narrow counters, where people stood and finished their food fast before making space for others.

The menu was painted on an old board, it was *Vaangibath* (Brinjal rice), *Chithranna* (Lemon rice) and *Bonda.*

"That's it?" Nethra asked.

"That's all you'll need," Baala replied.

"Order anything," said Gangayya. The range office will reimburse me."

Rishi tried to argue. "We'll pay"

"No no," Gangayya waved him off. "Don't insult a host."

Baala and Gangayya ordered two full plates of vangibath. The rest chose chitranna with bondas.

As they stood waiting, Nethra leaned closer to Sukhanya.

"Everyone's ordering something called… full figure?" she whispered.

Sukhanya raised an eyebrow. "What?"

Nethra turned to Gangayya. "What's this full figure they're asking for? It's not even on the menu."

Gangayya burst out laughing. "Oh, that's village English. Chitra means figure. So chitranna becomes 'figure rice.' Full plate is full figure, half plate is half figure."

The whole team cracked up.

"Imagine walking into a hotel and ordering a full figure!" Ibrahim joked.

Soon, their steaming hot plates arrived. The chithranna was tangy and peppered with mustard seeds and peanuts. The bondas were crisp on the outside, soft inside.

As they began to eat, two familiar faces walked into the hotel, holding hands to push through the crowd.

It was farmer Manjunatha and Pallavi.

The team waved. “Anna! Madam!”

“Heading to a housewarming today,” said Manjunatha. “No time to cook.”

Pallavi smiled warmly. “Have you all ordered, or shall we place it for you?”

“All done,” Gangayya replied.

Manjunatha nodded and moved to the counter to order.

“They look so happy,” murmured Nethra.

“Even with all the farm stress, they make time for each other,” Sukhanya added.

“Simple joys and that’s real love,” said Surya.

Their plates were wiped clean by the end. Not a grain remained. Bellies full, hearts warmer.

They climbed back into the jeep and began the bumpy ride to the range office. Mud puddles splashed. The team leaned against each other, dozing off to the rhythm of the road.

At the range office, they were ushered into a side room. Gangayya went in to meet the accounts officer and settle last month’s reimbursements.

The team waited, still discussing the morning’s events.

Suddenly, the calm was shattered.

Phones rang and officers shouted orders.

A staff member rushed out of the main office and came straight to Gangayya. "Gangayya, urgent situation and all ground staff required."

Gangayya's expression turned cold. He looked at the team.

"Everyone, into the jeep."

There was no hesitation. They grabbed their bags and bolted. The door slammed behind them as Baala revved the engine.

The jeep shot forward into the muddy forest trail.

Something serious had happened and they were heading straight into it.

SOMETHING SAD AND SOMETHING NEW

Baala's foot pressed heavy on the accelerator as the jeep roared to life and stormed down the muddy track. The team sat quietly in the back, bumping over the uneven terrain, all half-terrified and half-thrilled. Something serious had happened, that made even the usually unshaken Gangayya tighten his grip on the seat and look straight ahead without a word.

"What's going on?" Ibrahim finally whispered, his voice almost swallowed by the sound of the engine.

Gangayya didn't answer immediately. He pulled out his wireless set and spoke to someone, his tone clipped and urgent. After a few seconds, he turned around and said, "There's an injured leopard. Got caught in a snare set by poachers near the eastern beat. It's bad. We need to move fast."

The jeep skidded slightly as it took a sharp curve. The air was thick with tension.

They sped past the familiar bends of Chikkagundi's eastern boundary. As they neared the beat, signs of disturbance were evident with forest guards waving, a gathered crowd, murmurs of worry.

Baala brought the jeep to a halt near a narrow clearing. The students jumped down behind Gangayya, who was already striding toward a cluster of guards surrounding a low shrub patch.

Through the foliage, they spotted it a young leopard, his right foreleg twisted in a bike clutch wire, blood staining his golden rosetted fur. The animal hissed and snarled in pain, baring its teeth.

"Stand back," came a calm voice.

A woman stepped forward, her field shirt tucked in with quiet authority. A tranquilizer gun rested in her arms.

"Dr. Nikita," whispered Rishi.

She nodded briefly at the team, her eyes locked on the struggling leopard.

"The snare was likely set for wild hares," she said without looking away. "But it caught something much bigger."

She knelt low, loading the dart gun with practiced precision. "I'll need one clean shot. And absolute silence."

The forest seemed to hold its breath.

She fired and the dart struck the leopard's hindquarter. It let out a sharp cry, but the sedative worked quickly. Within moments, its breathing slowed, and the tension in its body released.

"Move in," Dr. Nikita called. Two guards approached with nets.

The students stood back, watching with awe and helplessness.

"It's a male, around three years," she confirmed after examining him. "The injury is serious, but treatable. We'll transport him to the nearest wildlife rehabilitation center."

The poacher's snare, now coiled and bagged, was folded and handed to one of the guards with instructions to submit it to the range office as evidence.

"Illegal traps have been increasing here," Dr. Nikita said. "Mostly for small game. But now, this."

As the vehicle with the sedated leopard pulled away, the students gathered around Dr. Nikita, still trying to process what they had witnessed.

"Will he be released back here?" Rishi asked.

"Yes," she said. "Once he's treated and recovers. That could take a couple of weeks, depending on how his wounds heal. We always release animals back into the area they were rescued from, unless it's unsafe."

Rishi hesitated, then asked, "But... how do you know how much sedative to use? You don't really know the exact weight of the animal in advance, right?"

Dr. Nikita smiled. "Good question. It's partly experience. Over time, you learn to estimate body mass based on size and age. But it's not just about the dosage. The temperature, the animal's stress level, even the environment matters too. If the surroundings are too noisy, or if the villagers gather and create a commotion, the animal can go into severe stress. That, combined with the sedation, can be fatal."

There was a sudden stillness in the group. The weight of the operation they had just witnessed now carried an even deeper gravity.

After a quick chat with Dr. Nikita about the leopard's rehabilitation and their own ongoing research, the team climbed back into the jeep. The ride to camp was subdued. The adrenaline had faded, leaving only thoughtfulness.

Soon after they reached the camp, lunch was served quietly and no one had much to say. The forest was silent, and it seemed respectful to match its mood.

Post lunch, the team decided to stay at the camp for the rest of the day. They brought out their notebooks and began segregating the data from the last few days.

It was then that Gangayya approached them, his face neutral but alert. "The ranger called. He asked if you all could organize one awareness program in Chikkagundi village. Something about snares, poaching... you know, what you saw today."

Before he could finish the sentence, Ibrahim had already said yes. Rishi and the others nodded eagerly.

"We'll do it," Sukhanya confirmed. "Day after tomorrow?"

Gangayya blinked in mild surprise. "That quick?" he chuckled. "Alright. I'll inform the ranger."

As he walked away, Rishi leaned back and said, "Back in Male Mahadeshwara Wildlife Sanctuary, I participated in one awareness event. The snares there were mostly set for deer."

He paused, then smiled. "We used a different approach there. You know, the sanctuary is named after Lord Mahadeshwara. It's believed he rides a tiger. So we explained to the villagers that, if you kill deer with snares, you're taking away the tiger's food. And since tiger is the lord's vehicle, harming its food chain is like disrespecting the lord himself."

Nethra raised an eyebrow. "That actually worked?"

"It did," Rishi said. "The number of snares dropped. Sometimes religious beliefs connect more deeply than facts."

That evening, after the sun had slipped behind the canopy, casting the camp in a quiet gold, the team roamed around the enclosures, checking on the elephants.

They helped the camp staff mix fodder, filled the water troughs, and even checked on the Sundra elephant

As the orange sky faded to twilight, they all gathered near the camp's central table, setting out sketchbooks and data sheets. Nethra lit a small lantern. "Let's plan the awareness content before dinner," she said.

Gangayya joined them later. "So," he said, "full day at the camp tomorrow. Then village duty the day after."

"Exactly," said Rishi. "We'll make sure it counts."

The forest hummed quietly in the background as the team scribbled, brainstormed, and prepared. A new mission awaited, but tonight, they were exactly where they belonged.

THE AWARENESS

After a day's planning, the sun had barely risen when the team began gathering near the camp kitchen, dressed in clean field clothes, their eyes still foggy with sleep. The smell of roasting spices drew them in like moths to a flame. There stood Gangayya, bent over a low stone stove, filtering thick tamarind juice through his fingers into a wide iron pan.

"Puliyogare today," he announced without looking up.

Puliyogare, fancily called tamarind rice in English, was anything but ordinary in these parts. It was a perfect harmony of sour, spicy, and nutty flavors. As the tamarind juice simmered with jaggery, red chilies, mustard seeds, and curry leaves, the kitchen filled with its inviting aroma. When mixed with warm rice and garnished with crunchy fried peanuts, it became an earthy, satisfying comfort dish.

"This tastes like it was made by someone who's cooked it a hundred times," Surya said, licking his fingers.

"Two hundred," Gangayya replied, smiling.

After breakfast, they loaded into the jeep and headed to Chikkadgundi village. Upon arrival, they were greeted by Mr. Dasappa, the village head, an elderly man in his 70s with a bright-white dhoti, a clean turban, and a deeply respected presence. It was said that if Dasappa spoke, the whole village listened.

He shook hands with Gangayya and welcomed the team warmly. After a short chat, he turned to two of his men and instructed, "Go call everyone to the panchayathi katte. Tell them it's important."

Within 20 minutes, around 120 villagers gathered under the giant banyan tree that stood in the heart of the village, its shade sprawling like a natural roof. Most of the crowd were young men in their 20s.

"Perfect," Rishi whispered. "The right age to shape thoughts."

Dasappa stepped forward and introduced the forest department officials, Gangayya and Baala and then the student team. A round of polite nods followed.

Rishi began the session, holding up a printed photo of the injured leopard. "This leopard was caught in a snare set in this very region. The wire cut deep into its leg. It could've died if not found in time."

A farmer's voice rose above the murmurs. "That same leopard took my dog two months ago!"

There were nods and grumbles of agreement. Several others began voicing similar concerns about livestock and crop damage.

The team quickly shifted approach and Ibrahim stepped in. "We understand your losses. But setting snares won't stop them. In fact, it makes things worse."

Anantha added, "When a snare kills a deer, the leopard loses its food. What does it do then? It comes looking for easier prey, your cattle and dogs."

Rishi took over. "And if a snare injures a predator, like in this case, it loses its hunting ability and it will stay near the village where prey is easier."

The logic settled over the crowd like fog. Heads began to nod.

But Rishi was conflicted. Deep down, he knew that wasn't the full scientific truth. The explanation they'd used was simple, but also simplified. Still, it worked and the villagers were now listening.

Dasappa raised a hand, calming the remaining murmurs. "Let us thank the team for coming, but I see many of you have more questions."

Voices rose again. "Elephants, leopards, losses…."

"This team isn't responsible for compensation," Dasappa said firmly. "I will speak to the DCF and call him here myself. For now, listen to these young people."

With that, the crowd slowly dispersed. Some lingered to thank the team. Dasappa, now smiling, gestured to the jeep.

"Come. I'll show you around the village."

He climbed into the front seat next to Baala, and the team hopped into the back. They first stopped at the sericulture sheds, humid structures lined with bamboo trays. Inside, soft white silkworms wriggled on heaps of mulberry leaves.

Dasappa explained the entire process from introducing the tiny worms into the shed to cocooning, harvesting, and drying.

Then they moved to a strange-looking farm, fields of dried, brittle-looking branches.

"That's odd," Nethra said. She plucked a tiny leaf. "Looks like hibiscus."

"Mulberry," Gangayya corrected. "Silkworm feed."

The branches were chewed bare. Barely any leaves remained.

"Chukke jinke," Dasappa said. "Spotted deer. They come every night and eat everything."

Gangayya's face fell. The team looked around and confirmed as deer pellets were scattered across the field.

Dasappa noticed Gangayya's silence. "Ayyo, I'm not blaming you. You're just the field man. I know who's responsible, it's the people eating up forest land. I'm just telling you what's happening."

The jeep rumbled on toward the village milk collection center. Stainless steel cans lined up as villagers queued to deposit milk. Dasappa explained how it was all sent to Mysuru's main dairy.

Next came a field completely trampled, the soil cracked and muddy.

"Elephants," Surya said instantly.

Dasappa nodded. "This was fodder for cattle. Gone overnight."

It became clear that Dasappa wasn't just giving a tour, but he was showing the pain points of every village farmer.

Then came the real moment of discussion.

"All this," Dasappa said, waving his hand across the fields, "because forests are shrinking. Politicians eat the land, and animals come out."

"If there's no food inside the forest," Ibrahim asked, "then why aren't all the elephants coming out?"

Rishi stepped in. "You're partly right, uncle. Yes, forest land is shrinking. But it's not that the forest doesn't have food. If that were true, all 20,000 elephants in the country would come out looking for food."

He paused. "They're not. Only a few herds like Sumangali's are coming out again and again. Why? Because they've developed a taste for your crops. It's like junk food for them."

"Like our samosas?" Surya joked.

"Exactly," Rishi smiled. "The forest is their proper meal. But crops are the samosas. They keep coming back even if it's not good for them."

Dasappa burst into laughter. "I haven't eaten junk food in my life. Only *ragi mudde* and some rice!"

Then he insisted, with grandfatherly authority, that they come home for lunch.

The team hesitated, but his insistence won. They followed him to his house which was a simple, clean, with red oxide floors and jasmine bushes at the entrance. While his wife and daughter prepared lunch, they sat outside.

Dasappa asked about their project, and they explained about Sumangali, calf positioning, and the trench gaps.

"Farmer Manjunatha mentioned this too," he said. "And the broken trench. I've seen Sumangali's herd many times, but not this year."

As they spoke, a young woman's voice called from inside, "Appaaa…"

"Lunch is ready," Dasappa said, standing. "Come. Let me introduce you."

Inside, Dasappa's wife served them steaming plates of ragi mudde and a flavorful vegetable saaru. As they settled down to eat, he introduced his shy daughter, Keerthishree, who had recently completed her M.Sc in Agriculture and they were now looking for a suitable match for her marriage.

The food was simple, earthy, and deeply satisfying. They even took a small serving of rice to complete the meal, because in the South, no meal feels finished without it.

After heartfelt thanks, the team boarded the jeep and returned to camp, full and tired.

Rishi said, "Let's avoid gaps in our fieldwork unless something urgent like the leopard case comes up." For which everyone agreed.

Baala and Gangayya nodded too. "Let's make every day count."

The team had returned to the camp, not just as students now, but as messengers between two worlds, where truth, trust, and a bit of tamarind rice could shift the balance.

THE NEWCOMERS

After weeks of uninterrupted fieldwork and multiple sightings of Sumangali's herd, the team found themselves in the middle of what felt like another slow, routine day. It had been three days since their last herd sighting. They drove quietly, scanning the forest on either side, when Gangayya's walkie-talkie crackled to life.

"Elephants spotted near Manjunatha's paddy field," came the urgent voice.

Without hesitation, Baala turned the jeep around and raced towards the location. Within minutes, they arrived near Manjunatha's farm, the team ready with their data sheets. The usual crowd of villagers, their screams and barking dogs echoed through the area.

The elephants, disturbed by the noise, had taken shelter in a nearby overgrown eucalyptus patch, about 200 meters from the field. The guards and trackers threw a couple of firecrackers into the thicket. Within seconds, the bush exploded with movement. Tails raised high, the elephants came charging out.

What unfolded next surprised everyone. It wasn't the usual composition. Instead of the familiar 7 adults plus 1 calf, they now saw 8 adults and 2 calves. The new calf was older, having crossed its mother's belly line, entering the juvenile phase.

Both calves tucked themselves under their respective mothers' bellies as the herd fled into the deeper forest. The urgency of their movement, especially with two young calves, puzzled the team.

Once the elephants disappeared, the team approached Manjunatha, who stood beside his wife, Pallavi, under the shade of a jackfruit tree. He recounted the incident.

"We were sitting here, discussing the pair of oxen we plan to buy. Suddenly, we heard branches breaking and within moments, ten elephants came into view. They looked confused, like they were trying to cross into the forest, but the village noise scared them into that eucalyptus patch."

Nethra, curious, asked, "Do you think they were using your farm as a corridor to reach the forest on the other side?"

Gangayya shook his head. "No, there's a well-connected stretch of forest behind. They might've just ventured out for some crop raiding. They found the nearest re-entry point and used it."

Manjunatha nodded. "They didn't touch the unripe bananas. Elephants go for the pith in the banana stems. But we acted quickly today. They didn't get the chance."

Rishi scribbled notes, his mind racing. The timing, the new additions, but something didn't fit. Why would a herd with two calves risk venturing into a village during daylight?

Curious about the entry and exit points, Rishi asked Gangayya to take them to the broken trench area inside the forest. They bid farewell to Manjunatha and Pallavi and drove into the forest.

Within ten minutes, they reached the spot where the elephants had presumably entered. Fresh tracks confirmed their suspicion. Rishi documented the trench breach and requested Baala to follow the tracks further into the forest, towards the direction where the elephants had exited.

The ride was bumpy but uneventful. About fifteen minutes in, they reached the boundary, but there was no trench here, only a solar fence.

To their surprise, the fence was partially broken and inactive.

"What happened here?" Rishi asked, turning to Gangayya.

"This was working fine until recently," Gangayya muttered. "I don't know what stopped the current."

He pulled out his walkie-talkie and requested the forest base to investigate the power disruption.

"I've got two broken barriers in my sector now," he murmured, concerned.

They resumed their search, following the tracks deeper into the forest.

Sukhanya turned to Gangayya. "Who are the new additions to the herd?"

"That's an identified female," Gangayya replied. "She used to be part of a herd of three. I don't know why she joined Sumangali's herd and she's got a calf with her now."

"How do you know it's her?" Ibrahim asked.

"She has a tear in her left ear. Very distinct."

They continued quietly until Baala stopped the jeep abruptly.

About 200 feet ahead stood Sumangali's herd, scattered and grazing. Baala slowly eased the vehicle forward, stopping 100 feet from the herd to avoid provoking a charge.

"Look! Look!" Gangayya whispered, pointing.

Sumangali's calf was suckling, not from its own mother, but from the new female.

Everyone sat in stunned silence.

The calves were easy to distinguish. The new calf was visibly older, around 16-18 months. Yet, the new female was calmly nursing Sumangali's younger calf. Sukhanya began filling out the behavioral data sheets and meanwhile surya jotted detailed notes.

"The new female has accepted the calf," Rishi murmured. "Fascinating. She's like an aunt now."

The team observed quietly as the herd slowly moved forward. They recorded the calf's distance from its mother, its behavior when stationary, and the adults' responses when the calf vocalized.

As the elephants disappeared into denser forest, the team stepped out and examined the area. They found fresh dung but no crop fibers, no ragi, no banana, indicating that the elephants hadn't fed in the village.

"Today was something else," Surya said, eyes wide.

"A perfect field day," Sukhanya added.

They would now need to revise their data sheets. The new female was designated Mother 2, and her calf noted as Calf 2. Though older and entering the juvenile stage, the calf still counted for their study.

Ibrahim, amused, asked, "So... we naming the calves now?"

Rishi turned, "Let's not. These are wild animals and we're here to study them, not domesticate their identity. Unless they become problematic and need management, they should remain nameless."

Everyone nodded in agreement.

The day had started as just another routine outing but ended as a goldmine of behavior and ecological insight. Two calves, two mothers, and new questions about elephant herd dynamics.

And now, they had one more mystery to unravel, why a lone mother from another herd was accepted into Sumangali's group, and what it meant for the social structures of wild Asian elephants.

BARRIERS

Following their earlier discussions and observations, the team immersed themselves deeper into their fieldwork. Data collection became more focused now, especially on understanding how barriers played a crucial role in mitigating human-elephant conflict. Since they had already studied trenches and solar-powered electric fences, they were keen on exploring other types of barriers used across different terrains.

During a break under the shade of a large banyan tree, Rishi brought it up, "We've seen two types of barriers, but I heard there are more. Gangayya, can we see them?"

Gangayya smiled and nodded. "You're lucky. My beat has almost all the different types of barriers used in this range. I'll show you one after the other."

Their first stop was in a sloping rocky patch of forest land. Trenches couldn't be dug here, nor could solar fences be fixed due to the uneven stone base. Instead, the Forest Department had built a rubbel wall.

The wall stood solid and intimidating, a thick, high structure of stones stacked uniformly, forming a continuous barrier. The construction technique ensured durability even in monsoon conditions. Elephants, though powerful, were discouraged by the wall's height and the rough stone texture, which made it impossible to climb or push down.

"These rubbel walls," Gangayya explained, tapping it with his stick, "are used in areas where digging is impossible. It's an old technique, but still very effective."

The team took all measurements and even noted the angle of the slope where the wall stood.

From there, they moved on to another location where instead of walls or trenches, the department had installed railway barrier fences.

“This one’s clever,” said Surya, observing the strong vertical beams.

Old, unused railway tracks had been repurposed and planted upright into the ground, close enough to block elephant entry, but spaced to allow human movement through footpaths in between.

“The department buys these unused tracks from the Railways at a cheaper price,” Gangayya added. “They’re heavy, strong, and last decades.”

The students observed how the iron beams resisted weathering, and the spacing strategy effectively prevented elephants from squeezing through. Rishi noted that these types of barriers also allowed seasonal movement of smaller animals.

The last stop for the day took them to a unique spot, a wide stream, roughly 40 feet across, that flowed gently between two forest patches. Here, the team was surprised to find a specially designed concrete structures.

“Here,” said Gangayya, “we couldn’t build anything like trenches, rubbel walls, or fences. So we built this.”

Five thick concrete pillars, each with a diameter of 1.5 meters, were erected in the stream. Spaced one meter apart, they allowed free flow of water while preventing elephants from wading across. The structure was both functional and eco-sensitive.

Rishi stared, impressed. “This needs civil engineering. Someone’s planned it in detail.”

"Yes," Gangayya nodded proudly. "It's not just forest officers, we need engineers, biologists like you all, wildlife vets and even IT experts."

As the team took notes, Gangayya folded his pants and stepped into the edge of the stream. "Let me try my luck with crabs," he grinned. But after a few minutes of poking around the muddy bank, he shook his head in disappointment. "Not today."

Everyone laughed as they climbed back into the jeep. The sun was already dropping behind the hills.

About 30 minutes into their return trail, Baala slowed the jeep and sniffed the air.

"Do you smell that?" asked Anantha, wrinkling his nose.

"Stop the jeep," Gangayya said sharply.

A foul, familiar odor filled the air, the unmistakable stench of death. As they listened, they could hear a loud buzzing sound. Flies. Gangayya stepped out and carefully moved toward the source of the smell. The team followed slowly, cautious but curious.

There it was, a half-eaten carcass of a male guar.

"A tiger's kill," Gangayya muttered, crouching near the body. "See how it's eaten? Started from the back...., classic tiger behavior."

"Could it be a leopard?" Sukhanya asked.

"No," he replied. "This is an adult guar which cannot be hunted down leopards."

Rishi bent down and inspected the kill. "These maggots are small. It's probably just few days-old kill."

Gangayya pointed to drag marks. "It hunted the guar there," he said, pointing to a spot a few meters away, "and dragged him here."

"Should we be worried the tiger's nearby?" Surya whispered.

"It might return to finish the kill, but tigers are shy. Still, let's not hang around for long," Gangayya said.

After taking quick GPS readings and notes, they backed out from the site and got back to the jeep.

As the sun dipped below the canopy, painting the forest in hues of gold and rust, the jeep rattled toward the camp.

Back in the safety of the camp, the students sat around sipping their hot tea. The day had been exhausting, but deeply insightful. As they watched the camp elephants heading towards the forest, a new idea emerged.

"We should create profiles of each camp elephant," suggested Nethra.

"Yes!" said Anantha. "Like ID cards, with their name, age, backstory, medical info…"

"And behavior traits," added Surya.

They began listing down what each profile could contain, excited at the thought. Though nothing was executed that evening, it was a plan and one they were eager to work on whenever free time permitted.

Under the starry sky, the forest settled into its nighttime rhythm. Crickets chirped, the wind whispered through the trees, and the team felt quietly grateful for the wild, the knowledge, and each other.

GOING WHERE AND WHY?

It had been a little over a month since the students had arrived at the Chikkagundi camp, and the rhythms of the forest had slowly seeped into their bones. That particular afternoon was unusually warm, even by late-September standards, autumn had quietly begun its descent, rustling the dry leaves and tinting the edges of the trees with a tired bronze. The sun sat lazily overhead, drenching everything in a dull gold.

Before lunch, as they sat outside, sipping tepid water from their bottles, Rishi wiped the sweat from his forehead and said, "Guys, we should call our parents, it's been over a week and they would be probably worrying."

"My mother's going to scream into the receiver first, and then cry," Nethra said with a small laugh.

"Only if she hears your voice before the phone cuts off," Surya smirked.

Sukhanya turned to Gangayya. "Anna, is there a coin booth somewhere nearby? We want to make a call home."

Gangayya scratched his beard. "Hmm... there's one near Manjunatha's farm, in that petty shop. Baala, let's take them."

They piled into the jeep and rolled down the winding mud road, past areca nut plantations. In fifteen minutes, they pulled up near the modest petty shop, the familiar smell of jaggery sweets and kerosene hitting them instantly.

The coin booth stood like a relic from another era, chipped paint, smudged glass, and a dangling receiver held together by faith and duct tape. One by one, they took turns calling their homes. The booth filled with mixed sounds of concern, affection, scolding, and relief.

Afterwards, out of courtesy, they walked over to Manjunatha's house. The farmer, with his grey beard and thick hands, was tending to his cattle when he saw them approach. He welcomed them with an enthusiasm that only genuine hearts possess.

"Oho! You came all this way and think I'll let you go without lunch?" he exclaimed. "Pallavi! Put some more rice on the stove!"

They protested lightly, but the smell of roasted spices already drifting from the kitchen sealed their fate. Within minutes, they were seated on red oxide floors, banana leaves spread before them. Pallavi, served them steaming hot rice, generous ladles of *hurli kaalu saar* (sprouted horse gram sambar), and cool curd.

"I don't know if I should eat or frame this meal," Surya whispered to Rishi as he bit into the smoky, earthy flavors.

The buttermilk came chilled, straight from a mud pot, with floating bits of green chili and ginger. As they drank it, the heat of the day retreated from their bodies.

Manjunatha leaned against a pillar and began chatting. "The elephants haven't come by in a while. But soon... within twenty days, they'll come for the jackfruits. Always do, like clockwork."

He pointed to the massive jackfruit tree in the backyard, its bark coarse and cracked with age. "Planted by my grandfather, over 95 years old. Four men needed to hug it. It still fruits like a youngster."

They nodded in admiration. Anantha scribbled notes in his field diary. As the food settled in their stomachs, a post-lunch laziness settled over them as the sun above was now a heavy lid on the world.

Gangayya finally stood. "Enough chitchat. Let's go see the herd. Baala, start the jeep."

They drove for fifteen minutes before Gangayya gestured for Baala to stop. "Stop here. About 200 meters ahead, they should be near the water body."

The students stood up slightly, peering ahead.

There they were, the herd. But surprisingly, not in the water. They were huddled close together under the sun, unusually still.

"No calves?" Sukhanya asked.

"Look closer," Gangayya whispered.

They scanned the herd, nestled under the bellies of the adult elephants were the calves, sleeping, stretched out on the ground. The mothers and aunts stood around them in a circle, their shadows forming a living umbrella.

"They're... giving them shade," Nethra whispered, astonished.

It was a picture of tenderness. The adults bore the brunt of the afternoon sun so the calves could sleep peacefully in the coolness of their shadows.

Moments later, Sumangali's calf stirred. With a gentle grunt, it stood and tottered toward her mother, who responded with a soft nudge and the calf began to suckle.

Then came the unexpected. The new calf approached its mother but didn't latch immediately. Instead, it gently rubbed its forehead against her teat, nudging, pressing, and rubbing, almost ritualistically.

"Why's it doing that?" Rishi wondered aloud.

"Second time I'm seeing this," Gangayya said quietly. "Years ago, from a different herd, but no one really knows."

Rishi, half-serious, said, "Maybe it's stimulating milk flow?"

Behind him, Ibrahim and Surya exchanged a look, their faces cracking into secret grins.

"What?" Sukhanya narrowed her eyes.

"Nothing," they chorused too quickly.

As the calves woke and began their little games, mock charges, trunk tugs, and muddy rolls, the students took detailed notes: distances from the herd, duration of suckling, play patterns.

Sumangali's calf, as usual, grew restless and annoyed its mother. When it tried to suckle again, Sumangali moved forward, denying her. The calf stood still, watching the new mother.

With a bold move, the calf walked over and latched onto the new mother. Surprisingly, the new mother didn't resist.

"That's... aunt love," Ananth murmured.

They watched silently, overcome by the bonds of kinship, understanding that elephants didn't operate as individuals but as families with memory, feeling, and social rules.

After an hour, the herd started moving, heading towards the jeep.

Baala cranked the engine and slowly reversed, keeping respectful distance. The elephants moved left and disappeared into the woods.

"We'll wait a bit, then head to the water," Gangayya said.

Soon after, they stepped near the water body, splashing their faces to shake off drowsiness. But the banks were muddy.

"Too risky here," Gangayya warned. "This place is deceptive. Muddy at the edge and deep inside. We'll go to another spot."

Just then, his walkie-talkie crackled.

A voice came through: "*Campge barbeku, selection aagbeku.*" (You need to come back to the camp and selection has to be done.)

Gangayya stiffened slightly. Ibrahim, sharp as ever, asked, "Selection? For what?"

Gangayya gave a half-smile. "You'll know when we reach."

Surya frowned. "Where are they going?"

"Some of the elephants have to leave," Gangayya said cryptically, adjusting the volume on the walkie.

The jeep started, but the silence inside it was now heavy. A knot of worry had started forming.

Where were the elephants going?

And more importantly, why?

AND SO, DISAPPOINTMENT STARTED

As they began their journey back to the camp, Rishi, unable to suppress his curiosity, turned to Gangayya. "Sir, can we revisit the gaur carcass site we went to the other day? It's just a few minutes away."

Gangayya nodded, and Baala adjusted the steering to take a detour. As they approached the spot, an overpowering stench filled the air, worse than before. Flies buzzed around in greater numbers, and the carcass had deteriorated considerably. The skin was now sloughing off in sheets, hanging grotesquely from bones, and the stench of decay was almost unbearable. Maggots writhed over the exposed flesh, and it was clear that the tiger had returned, intestines had been dragged out and half-eaten. The students quickly jotted down their observations, their faces showing a mix of intrigue and discomfort. Without wasting more time, they left the site and headed directly to the camp.

Once at the camp, they noticed Dr. Nikita's jeep parked in the shade. She was already seated on a mat under a tree, casually eating her lunch. The team joined her, tired but glad for a break.

During lunch, Nethra turned to Gangayya and asked, "Why is Dr. Nikita here today? And what's happening with the elephants?"

Gangayya wiped his mouth with his scarf before answering. "The Dasara festival is coming. Elephants from different camps across the state are being selected and moved to Mysuru for the event. They'll be gone for about three months."

The students sat up straighter, glancing at each other in surprise. It dawned on them that the famed Mysuru Dasara was just forty days away. As children of Mysuru, this festival had been a regular part of their lives, vibrant processions, caparisoned elephants, music, lights, and a celebration of the city's culture and history.

Dasara, also known as Navaratri, had roots tracing back to the reign of the Wodeyar kings, who dedicated it to Chamundeshwari Devi, the presiding deity of Mysuru. The highlight of the festival is the grand procession on Vijayadashami, where the lead elephant carries the golden howdah holding the idol of the goddess.

As the team digested both the food and this sudden information, they overheard another tracker speaking to Dr. Nikita. He was discussing a troublesome wild elephant from an adjoining range. "He's been raiding crops and recently injured a farmer. The ranger has written to the DCF seeking permission to capture him." The tracker added, "He's got thick tusks and good height. If captured and trained well, he'll make a perfect addition to the Dasara lineup."

The students exchanged glances, a mix of disbelief and discomfort spreading across the group. Murmurs began, "Why would a tracker say something like that?" Surya whispered. "Isn't he supposed to protect wild elephants?"

Sukhanya frowned. "They could try relocating him to a less conflict-prone area. Why assume he should serve a human tradition?"

"Exactly," Rishi muttered. "We keep removing these tusked males… it could affect breeding rates. And it's ironic that we encroach on their forests, neglect to maintain barriers, and then punish them for reacting."

Though no one said it aloud, a collective disappointment hung in the air. They finished their lunch in silence, washed their plates, and followed Dr. Nikita, who was preparing to head out to the next camp.

Dr. Nikita turned to the students. "Can you all help me compile a profile file for the two female elephants from this camp? They'll be going to Mysuru."

The students nodded eagerly as they had already planned to do it.

"Are they the ones who flank the main tusker during the procession?" Anantha asked.

"Yes," Dr. Nikita confirmed. "They're experienced, well-behaved females. Important to the formation."

She then proceeded with a quick health checkup on both elephants, explaining to the students what needed to be recorded: age, dental health, foot condition, temperament, weight, and signs of musth in males, though in this case, it was just the two females. She instructed the mahouts to bathe the elephants and prepare them for travel by the end of the day. With that, she took the profile file and left swiftly, needing to reach the next camp to oversee the selection of male elephants.

As the students wrapped up the profiles, the air around them still felt heavy from the earlier conversation. The tracker's words lingered like an unsettling echo.

Suddenly, Gangayya's walkie-talkie crackled to life. A voice came through: "Your herd… and Sumangali… come immediately to the sugarcane field near the abandoned farmland."

Everyone froze.

"The herd again?" Surya asked.

Gangayya gave a curt nod. "Looks like they've moved through the abandoned land again."

The team grabbed their data sheets and hopped into the jeep. Despite the seriousness of the situation, there was a spark of excitement that they might get to observe the herd navigating the landscape themselves.

As they neared the sugarcane fields, they were greeted by a large crowd. The atmosphere buzzed with tension. But oddly, the crowd wasn't looking towards the abandoned farm land, where they knew the herd was hiding in the bushes.

Instead, all heads were turned in the opposite direction.

What were they looking at?

The answer waited in the unfolding chaos ahead.

THE DAY WE FAILED

The crowd wasn't facing the abandoned land where the herd was supposed to be. Instead, all eyes were fixed on the sugarcane field. Tension crackled in the air like a storm about to break.

The team pushed their way through the crowd, hearts pounding, uncertain of what lay ahead. As they broke past the final row of villagers, they froze.

There, at the edge of the sugarcane field, an elephant lay collapsed on her knees, her legs tucked under her like she was kneeling in prayer. Her calf wandered nearby, confused and distressed.

It was Sumangali.

"Oh no," whispered Nethra.

Gangayya stepped forward slowly, with a voice like dry leaves crushed underfoot,

"It's all over."

A stunned silence fell over the team.

Shock rippled through them. Surya gritted his teeth, anantha covered his mouth and sukhanya clutched Rishi's arm, her knuckles pale.

In the distance, the local forest ranger was seen dragging the sugarcane field owner toward a jeep. The farmer looked ashamed, terrified. Gangayya approached the man's younger brother, an old friend.

The younger man, clearly shaken, began to explain.

"My brother set up live electric wires around the field to stop the elephants. I begged him not to but he said it wouldn't kill one, just scare them away. It was meant to be on only at night... but..."

He choked and tears welled in his eyes.

"The herd had already crossed back over the fence. But one was still inside. My brother saw it... and without thinking, he switched on the current. She tried to cross and fell... just like that. Then he turned it off, panicking... but it was too late."

The crowd murmured as the truth sank in. The calf had remained behind, pacing near Sumangali's still body. The herd had tried to return, but the noise and chaos of the villagers had driven them away.

"He didn't mean it, Gangayya," the brother pleaded. "Please, don't let them punish him. He didn't know."

Rishi stepped forward, voice trembling but firm. "It doesn't matter, elephants are protected animals and killing them is a punishable offense, this is a crime."

Gangayya held up a hand. "Nobody speaks another word, not here and not now. This is too volatile."

Within minutes, a team of forest officials from nearby ranges began to arrive. Ibrahim's uncle, the ACF, followed. Then, just twenty minutes later, the DCF arrived, barking orders. The villagers were pushed 500 meters away, the farmer was arrested and the electrified wires were removed and stacked into a waiting jeep.

A JCB rumbled onto the field to dig a pit.

Everything moved with eerie efficiency, like a procedure they had practiced before.

Mahouts from the camp arrived, accompanied by Veera, the tusker. Veera stood near the entrance to the abandoned land, ready to prevent the herd from returning. He was the barrier between grief and conflict.

Meanwhile, five men moved toward the calf.

It was heart-wrenching to see the calf calling out in distress, circling Sumangali's body, nudging her, waiting for her to rise.

But she would never stand again.

The calf cried louder and this time, the herd responded. From the abandoned land, the new female led a hesitant attempt to return.

Veera stepped forward and blocked their path, gently but firmly. The new female challenged him briefly, lifting her trunk, rumbling. Veera replied with a commanding head-to-head nudge, pushing them back into the scrub.

His mahout followed, guiding the herd deeper into the forest.

Back in the field, ropes were slipped around the calf. She resisted, cried, but she was no match. They lifted her into a mini truck, tied her securely, and drove her to the elephant camp.

Moments later, Dr. Nikita arrived.

The DCF and the ranger conferred with her quickly. The cause of death was clear and there would be no postmortem.

The JCB driver began digging the grave.

Sukhanya, unable to hold back any longer, began to cry. The others gathered around her, trying to offer comfort.

On one side lay the lifeless body of the elephant they had studied, revered. On the other, her calf, now orphaned.

Rishi's thoughts churned. "*Why was the calf taken to the camp? Why not reunited with the herd?*" He looked toward the DCF and Dr. Nikita, wanting to speak, but their faces were hard with focus. Now wasn't the time.

The grave was soon ready. A few villagers asked to perform a pooja. They were allowed and joined by the rangers and the team, hands folded, eyes downcast.

When the JCB began to push Sumangali into the pit, a wave of horror passed through the team. She looked so peaceful, yet so wrong.

One moment she was a gentle giant serving the nature. The next, just another body returned to the soil.

Soon, the pit was filled and flattened.

The DCF approached them. "I will speak with you soon. I need to talk to Pranay about what happens next."

Rishi still couldn't speak as his throat held his protest like a stone.

Four hours, that was all it took for Sumangali's life to end and for a family to shatter.

As they drove back, they passed Veera and his mahout.

"They've gone back into the forest," the mahout said. "But I think they'll come back in the night. They'll want to check again."

Rishi murmured, more to himself than anyone else:

"They will come back. Why wouldn't they? They lost two family members today."

Back at camp, they found Dr. Nikita beside the calf, trying to calm her.

The team had questions.

"Why was Sumangali buried in the field?" asked Surya.

Dr. Nikita sighed. "Because it was the farmer's crime, there's nothing wrong with burying her at the crime site."

She looked at the calf and added, "It's sad that she had to end up here. We've tried raising orphaned calves before, but they didn't survive. But this time, we're calling in a senior biologist, Ms. Chandana. She's raised orphaned wildlife successfully before. If there's anyone who can help, it is her."

Rishi stepped forward. "But the calf could've gone back to the herd. There was another nursing female. She even tried to come back for the calf."

Dr. Nikita paused. Her face changed.

"What? Are you sure?"

The whole team nodded.

"She kept trying to approach when the calf called out," Anantha confirmed.

Dr. Nikita immediately pulled out her phone and called the DCF.

"I need to tell him now, maybe we still have time."

Then, she turned to the team. "Can you also inform Mr. Pranay? If we act quickly, maybe... maybe... we can try and send this little one back to the wild."

Hope flickered.

CAN WE STILL CALL HER WILD?

It was past 8 in the night, and the camp was quiet except for the soft rustling of eucalyptus leaves and the occasional distressed trumpet of the calf.

Dr. Nikita had been asked to stay back at the camp and observe the calf until Ms. Chandana arrived from Mysuru, she had already informed Nikita about the kind of enclosure the mahouts were to construct, and even before her arrival, the mahouts had begun building the structure using small-sized eucalyptus logs, working under the yellow flicker of lanterns and a looming sense of urgency.

Inside the temporary shed, the calf refused the bottle of milk offered by the students, she only responded with constant, helpless distress calls that echoed painfully through the night, and the sound struck the team in a way no data or documentation ever could.

Soon, Pranay called Dr. Nikita to ask for updates. She spoke briefly and then handed the phone over to Rishi, knowing that no one understood this herd better than him. Rishi, with calm determination, explained the calf's background, the sightings, the second nursing female who had clearly shown intent to care, and urged Pranay to speak to the DCF and at least attempt a reunion.

Pranay, though unsure, agreed to try and discuss it, and after a thoughtful pause, hung up the call.

Outside, Gangayya lit a small fire and called everyone for dinner, not that anyone was hungry, but they still served their plates with a little food and gathered around the warmth, speaking little, rotating turns to sit near the calf while others ate, all of them silently grieving the calf's situation.

After dinner, the team sat near the calf with Dr. Nikita, sharing field stories of the calf, each story a thread connecting their hearts to her.

Suddenly, headlights appeared in the dark, and a black Bolero rolled into camp, ranger Rajappa stepped out, followed by Ms. Chandana, who wasted no time, she headed straight to the calf, her presence firm yet gentle, instructing the mahouts to untie all the ropes around the calf, save for a light one on the hind limb, which too would be removed once the enclosure was ready.

Rajappa introduced the students to Chandana and told her that they had been studying this calf and her mother for the past two months. Then, Dr. Nikita added the details of the events that led to the separation and conveyed what Rishi had said about the possibility of a reunion.

Chandana listened patiently and said that if a chance to reunite the calf arose, it must be tried, but the decision ultimately lay with the DCF. If a reunion wasn't possible, the calf would have to be raised here under their care, and then she moved swiftly to the enclosure where the mahouts were still working, giving them precise instructions on design, comfort, and hygiene.

As it was getting late, some of the students retired to bed, physically exhausted and emotionally drained, while Rishi and Sukanya chose to stay with the calf. They laid out their mats in the same room, not too close to disturb her, but close enough so she wouldn't feel alone.

Dr. Nikita too returned to her shared quarters, and once Chandana had reviewed everything, she also joined Nikita in the same room, leaving Rishi and Sukanya sitting in silence by the calf, as the rhythmic clinking of beer bottles being carried in a black plastic cover by Rajappa and his driver Shiva faded into the night behind the quarters.

Sukanya, glancing from the window, watched them disappear into the shadows and murmured, "*Everyone's slipping back into their routines, pretending this is just another case... but we're making a mistake, a big one, by not trying to reunite her.*"

The night passed slowly, filled with the soft thud of logs being arranged, the occasional snores of tired mahouts, and the constant, aching calls of the calf.

Soon after sunrise, the rumble of another jeep announced the arrival of the DCF and scientist Pranay. Within ten minutes, the whole team, unshowered and anxious, gathered near the calf's temporary holding room as the DCF stepped in, his face stern but unreadable.

Chandana gave him an update and led the entire group to the newly built enclosure. It was a spacious room constructed using dry eucalyptus logs, ventilated carefully to maintain airflow without losing warmth, with a secondary inner cabin made of smaller eucalyptus stems, a flooring of hay and mud, and a pile of jute sacks arranged to serve as bedding.

The DCF inspected the structure silently and then stepped outside where Chandana and Nikita explained the potential reunion plan, the lingering herd, the second female, and the possible acceptance based on behavior and maternal response.

The DCF listened but remained unmoved. With a deep sigh, he said, "We've tried this before... when an orphaned calf was reintroduced, the herd turned hostile, aggression broke out, and we almost lost that calf. If that happens again, it won't just be a failure, it will be a tragedy."

"But sir," Rishi interjected quietly, "we have experienced staff, trained kumki elephants, we could manage it better this time… why not give it a try?"

The DCF turned to him and said, "I understand, but I don't want to take that risk in this case and this calf stays with us."

The room fell into a thick, heavy silence, no one dared speak, but the pain in their eyes said everything.

Pranay and Dr. Nikita both looked at the students with guilt, they had hoped for a different outcome, but their hands were tied, and the moment passed like a cold wave through the room.

The students felt their hearts sink, not just because the reunion had been denied, but because it hadn't even been tried. Their minds swirled with regret that they hadn't spoken directly to the DCF in the field, though deep down they knew that perhaps it wouldn't have changed anything.

The DCF then instructed Chandana to design a care plan for the calf and told Pranay to inform the students about the next steps in their project, and without a moment's pause, he climbed back into the jeep and drove away.

Chandana, ever composed, got to work immediately. She drafted a meticulous plan that included scheduled feeding, enrichment, hygiene measures, no access policies and many more.

She handed the supply list to Rajappa and insisted it be arranged before nightfall.

Despite their efforts, the calf continued to let out soft, aching distress calls, which echoed into the surrounding forest. The team stood outside, unable to step inside, watching helplessly as the calf stumbled between hay and wall, her ears twitching at every sound.

Chandana reassured the team that they would be allowed to see her occasionally, "It's about hygiene… but I know how much you care," she said gently.

She, though composed and professional, paused at the entrance of the enclosure and watched the calf longer than necessary, her eyes reflecting the same silent question everyone else had been asking deep inside.

Rishi looked on, Sukanya clutched her notebook to her chest, Nethra wiped a quiet tear, and Gangayya just stood still with his arms crossed and eyes low.

None of them spoke, because they were all thinking the same thing, if we isolate her from the very world she came from, then…

Can we still call her wild?

.

.

.

To be continued…

SCIENTIFIC NAMES

FAUNA

1. **Barn Owl-** ***Tyto alba***
2. **Black Kite-** ***Milvus migrans***
3. **Black Rhino-** ***Diceros bicornis***
4. **Cicada-** ***Rustia minuta***
5. **Crab-** ***Spiralothelphusa hydrodroma***
6. **Dhole-** ***Cuon alpinus***
7. **Dung Beetle-** ***Copris indicus***
8. **Guar-** ***Bos gaurus***
9. **Grey Hornbill-** ***Ocyceros birostris***
10. **Grey Langur-** ***Semnopithecus entellus***
11. **Hare-** ***Lepus nigricollis***
12. **Housefly-** ***Musca domestica***
13. **Indian Elephant-** ***Elephas maximus indicus***
14. **Indian Flying Fox-** ***Pteropus giganteus***
15. **Jungle Babbler-** ***Argya striata***
16. **Jungle Crow-** ***Corvus macrorhynchos***
17. **Leopard-** ***Panthera pardus***
18. **Marsh Crocodile-** ***Crocodylus palustris***
19. **Myna-** ***Acridotheres tristis***
20. **Nightjar-** ***Caprimulgus asiaticus***
21. **Peafowl-** ***Pavo cristatus***
22. **Rose Ringed Parakeet-** ***Psittacula krameri***
23. **Sloth Bear-** ***Melursus ursinus***
24. **Spectacled Cobra-** ***Naja naja***
25. **Spotted Deer-** ***Axis axis***
26. **Tiger-** ***Panthera tigris***
27. **Wild Boar-** ***Sus scrofa***

FLORA

1. **Arjuna-** ***Terminalia arjuna***
2. **Bamboo-** ***Bambusa bambos***
3. **Eucalyptus-** ***Eucalyptus globulus***
4. **Jackfruit-** ***Artocarpus heterophyllus***
5. **Jamun-** ***Syzygium cumini***
6. **Lantana-** ***Lantana camara***
7. **Mango-** ***Mangifera indica***
8. **Rain Tree-** ***Samanea saman***
9. **Shorea-** ***Shorea robusta***
10. **Tamarind-** ***Tamarindus indica***
11. **Teak Tree-** ***Tectona grandis***
12. **Tulsi-** ***Ocimum tenuiflorum***

REFERENCES

The Mating and the Miracle

Jue Jue, Zaw Min Thant, Shozo Shibata. GPS tracking reveals home range and habitat preference of semi-captive elephants in Myanmar. *Landscape and Ecological Engineering.* (2024) 20:213-221

Thomas B.H., Imke Lueders, Robert Hermes, Frank Goeritz, Joseph Saragusty. Reproductive cycle of the elephant. *Animal Reproductive Science.* (2011) 124 176-183

Hodges JK. Endocrinology of the ovarian cycle and pregnancy in the Asian (Elephas maximus) and African (Loxodonta africana) elephant. *Animal Reproduction Science.* (1998) 53(1-4):3-18.

de Silva S, Webber CE, Weerathunga US, Pushpakumara TV, Weerakoon DK, Wittemyer G. Demographic variables for wild Asian elephants using longitudinal observations. *PLoS One.* (2013) 20;8(12):e82788.

Garstang M. Long-distance, low-frequency elephant communication. *J Comp Physiol A Neuroethol Sens Neural Behav Physiol.* (2004) 190(10):791-805.

Beeck, V.C., Heilmann, G., Kerscher, M. *et al.* A novel theory of Asian elephant high-frequency squeak production. *BMC Biology.* (2021) 19, 121.

Between Giants and Gateways

Manigandan K, Maria Anjum, Ramakrishnan Balasundaram, Avinash Krishnan. Patterns and determinants of human-elephant